Up 2 Cents a Share Down 8 Million Jobs

Up 2 Cents a Share
Down 8 Million Jobs

How Immigration, Politics, and Greed
are Destroying the American Workforce

Dan Geoffrey

iUniverse, Inc.
New York Lincoln Shanghai

Up 2 Cents a Share Down 8 Million Jobs
How Immigration, Politics, and Greed are Destroying the American Workforce

iUniverse, Inc.

For information address:
iUniverse, Inc.
2021 Pine Lake Road, Suite 100
Lincoln, NE 68512
www.iuniverse.com

ISBN: 0-595-32711-7

Printed in the United States of America

Contents

Introduction

Millions of people are entering into the United States each year illegally. They enter the United States without jobs, and have become an overwhelming burden on the economy.

The United States spends hundreds of millions of dollars each year in health care costs, alone, taking care of many illegal immigrants who enter the country and who do not have health care insurance.

The weight of this burden falls on the shoulders of every citizen in this country. Tens of millions of our citizens work and pay taxes each day, cannot afford health care insurance. In short, although health care is provided to illegal immigrants, little effort is made to ensure that our own citizens are covered.

For many people, an illness can be financially devastating. Afraid of losing all that they have worked for in case they get sick, elderly people often put their homes in their children's names. Children who should be receiving medical care do not because their parents cannot afford to pay for it. It is hardly surprising that so many people feel they would be better off on welfare because, at least they (and their children) would not have to worry about getting care in the event of illness or injury.

Our school systems are overburdened. Programs are being cut because of the lack of funds. A child in a woodworking class may be unable to work on any projects because there is not enough money available to buy wood.

People have put their homes up for sale because they can no longer afford to pay taxes. If you want a small education, next time you are at the gas station look closely at the sign on the pump. Not that long ago, gasoline was $1.50 a gallon, but at least 50 cents of that cost goes to cover state and federal taxes. With 1/3 of the price of a gallon of gas going toward taxes, states should be running heavily in the black. Instead, they are broke.

In the last few years, there has been a lot of speculation about the impact of immigration on the U.S. economy. The immigrant population is increasing at such an alarming rate that the future absorption of tens of millions of immigrants into our economy is now only a best guess scenario. The issue is not whether we will be able to handle the additional population, but rather how this staggering increase will affect our lives.

Take a look at the housing industry. Housing costs have doubled and will likely continue to increase while fewer and fewer affordable homes are available. For the moment, the rate of home ownership is up largely because interests rates are down. If interest rates go up, however, home ownership rates will drop accordingly.

Because of immigration, salaries are likely to remain low. If the cost of housing continues to rise, the next generation may be unable to purchase homes.

I'm sure there's room and time here to argue. I know there's time, because the retirement age keeps rising.

http://www.census.gov/
From the Subjects A-Z, select the desired topic

The following information from U.S. Census

Health Care Insurance—2002 data

- 43.6 million people did not have health care insurance up 2.4 million from 2001
- People age 18–24 were less likely to have health care insurance
- 10.5 million poor people or 30.4 percent of people in poverty had no health care insurance of any kind

Population

- Total Population 1990—248,709,873
- Total Population 2000—281,421,906
- Total Population 2003—290,809,777

Poverty Rate

- 2002 poverty rate 12.1% 34.6 million people
- 2nd consecutive year increase
- 2001 poverty rate 11.7%

Income

- Median HOUSEHOLD income—$42,409 representing a 1.1% real decline from 2001 level of $42,900

From 1990 to the year 2003, the population increased by ~42 million people. Projections for 10 years not including a new immigration policy/amnesty would bring the population to ~ 330 million people.

The population is increasing by over 40 million people every ten years. What will we do when the population exceeds our ability to absorb the immigrant populations to whom we are opening our doors? The statistical data above is only a prelude to what we can expect in the future.

Far from working for us, our politicians have their own agenda, which largely revolves around getting and staying elected. That takes lots of money, the kind that can only come from special interest groups, corporations, wealthy contributors, and/or foreign governments.

Using the Freedom of Information Act (FOIA), I was able to obtain a CD-ROM containing all the 2003 H-1B Labor Conditions Application Data. From the Assistant Secretary of the Department Labor, I also requested and received a list of the top 100 companies hiring H-1Bs.

The data on the CD was in MS Access format. When I dragged the two files onto my desktop and opened them, I thought my computer was going to have a stroke. The first database was close to 200MB and the second about 65MB.

These weren't just the top 100 companies. I had every application for certification (including the companies that hired them, contact information, salaries to be paid, etc.)

Ostensibly, H-1B non-immigrant visas were created to fill positions left vacant by shortages of skilled labor in the United States. In spite of our vast resources as a nation, apparently we were unable to fill the following positions, listed by state.

State	Position
AK	Fishing boat deck hand
AK	Head Women's Basketball Coach
AK	Motel Manager
AL	Assistant Women's Volleyball Coach
AL	Assistant Food Service Director
AL	Head Women's Soccer Coach
AZ	Accountant
CA	Art Director
CA	Teacher
CA	Web Designer
CT	Sales Manager
CT	Gymnastics Instructor
FL	Manager/Food Service

The rampant abuse of this program is clear. For many colleges, universities, and states this program is little more than a placement agency. With millions of Americans looking for work, companies are going overseas to find motel managers, gymnastics instructors, sales managers, accountants, teachers, engineers, etc. What is wrong with the picture?

If you feel as though you are being pushed overboard, it is because you are!

Finally, throughout this book web site links to federal reports, regulations, and statistics are cited. If you have any doubt as to the authenticity of what is written here, please check these web sites and read the material in its entirety for yourself.

Chapter 1
History of the H-1B Visa

Let me say, at the beginning, that I have no doubt that many people have benefited from the H-1B training grants program and that many companies have provided excellent opportunities for American workers to enhance their skills under these grants. In the end, perhaps the H-1B program is just a good example of The Law of Unintended Consequences.

American businesses had been complaining of shortages in the workforce in certain areas such as high technology for some time. To address this issue, Congress passed the Immigration Act of 1990, which took effect in 1992. Designed to help companies access skilled foreign labor and facilitate international competition, this act established an H-1B visa category for non-immigrants who wanted to work in high skill/high technology areas. Only 65,000 people were allowed to enter the United States through this program each year.

It was not long, however, before the annual limits were increased to 115,000 a year by 1998 and to 195,000 a year by the year 2000. A $500.00 user fee was imposed on companies for each person they intended to bring in under this program. That fee was later raised to $1,000 for each person brought in under an H-1B.

In effect, Congress had just made it possible for corporations to find skilled labor outside the United States while at the same time millions of people, many of them recent college graduates, were searching for employment.

It is, at the least, infuriating to realize that several hundred thousand jobs a year are being taken by foreign workers to satisfy the so-called "Skilled Labor Shortage" in the United States, unless of course you really believe that this country cannot produce enough graduates to meet the needs of American companies. Far more likely, the so-called shortage was merely a smoke screen to allow American companies easy access to cheap labor. Companies specifically sought people with Bachelor's and/or Master's Degrees, and doctorates. Most of these jobs were to fill computer-related or information technology positions.

It must be noted, however, that under the American Competitiveness and Workforce Improvement Act (ACWIA), over $300 million (or 56.3 per cent of the user fees imposed on the companies) would be collected for re-training American workers to help them become more competitive. Using those funds to re-train American workers was a pretty good idea, although allowing the DOL to decide who would receive the training was not so good.

Seventy-five percent of the funds would be provided through competitive bidding to local workforce investment boards. The remaining twenty-five percent would go to those who met certain partnering requirements.

If the fees collected amounted to over $300 million, then that would mean a greater easing of the burden on American taxpayers. Of course, under the H-1B rule, approximately 200,000 jobs a year were still being filled by foreign workers, which meant that in 5 years 1,000,000 American jobs were effectively lost.

The DOL was assigned the responsibility of administering the ACWIA grants. Decisions were made based on assigned points in six different areas. Those who scored the most points got the grants. No grant award could exceed $3 million.

The H-1B grants in conjunction with the ACWIA could have become one of the best federal programs ever devised. Here, finally, was a program to help people acquire the skills they needed to work. An added bonus was that program participants could be employed or unemployed during the training.

Yet, if this was, indeed, a "win-win" situation for both employers and employees, why were corporations still laying off workers and outsourcing or permanently transferring jobs to other countries?

Something about the data started to bother me that I just couldn't figure out what about the information I was seeing was wrong. I saw some very large corporations who were laying off employees in the New England area. Some of the corporations were permanently sending jobs to Mexico while other positions were being outsourced.

You might think that these companies would be aggressively seeking ways to re-train their workers.

Yet, statistics from the DOL web site showed that many companies were still outsourcing jobs and laying off workers even as they applied for permission, under the H-1B regulations, to bring foreign workers into this country. That can't be possible. The government wouldn't let a company apply for a training grant when they are laying off and moving jobs outside the U.S. They wouldn't let a company apply for a training grant if they are applying to get people from other countries to work in the U.S. Not only could they apply, they could receive millions of dollars in funding.

Just think about how awesome this really is. You layoff workers or outsource, you hire foreign workers to fill American jobs and then you receive a training grant from the United States Department of Labor to train workers so they can compete with foreign labor.

Not only did I find one company, but I found multiple companies taking part in these grant programs that were doing exactly this. In fact, some of the companies had brought workers into the United States to be trained and then sent them back to Mexico with the job of the worker that trained them. The same companies were receiving federal money to train their workforce to be more competitive.

If there was ever a case where "there ought to be a law," this is certainly one of them.

Is it at least reasonable to suppose that companies that receive worker-training grants will no longer feel it necessary to look outside the U.S. for skilled labor? The answer is, yes, it is reasonable to suppose that. You would, however, be wrong. Not just companies, but also local and state governments, school systems, and many other organizations, which have received worker-training grants, have also submitted hundreds of H-1B applications for permission to bring in foreign workers to fill American jobs.

Leading Employers of Specialty Occupation Workers (H-1B):
October 1999 to February 2000
U.S. Immigration and Naturalization Service (INS)
June 2000
http://uscis.gov/graphics/shared/services/employerinfo/h1top100.pdf

The following, is the list of the top 100 (actually 102 companies) companies participating in the program;

Leading Employers of Specialty Occupation Workers (H-1B) October 1999 to February 2000. U.S. Immigration and Naturalization Service June 2000. Table reproduced from this report.

Rank	Company	Number	Rank	Company	Number
1	Motorola	618	16	Tekedge Corp	219
2	Oracle Corp	455	17	Data Conversion	195
3	Cisco Systems Inc 398		18	Tata Infotech	185
4	Mastech	389	19	Cotelligent	183
5	Intel Corp	367	20	Sun Microsystems Inc	182
6	Microsoft Corp	362	21	Compuware Corp	179
7	Rapidigm	357	22	KPMG LLP	177
8	Syntel Inc	337	23	Intelligroup	161
9	Wipro LTD	327	24	Hi Tech Consultants Inc	157
10	Tata Consultancy Serv	320	25	Group Ipex Inc	151
11	PriceWaterhouseCoopers LLP	272	26	Ace Technologies Inc	149
12	People Com Constultants Inc	261	27	Hewlett Packard Co	149
13	Lucent Technologies	255	28	Everest Consulting GR	147
14	Infosys technologies LTD	239	29	Bell Atlantic Network Serv	141
15	Nortel Networks Inc	234	30	Ernst Young LLP	137

Rank	Company	Number	Rank	Company	Number
31	Aglient Technologies Inc	136	67	MSI Majesco Software Inc	80
32	Deloitte Touche LLP	130	68	Data Core Systems	78
33	Birlasoft	128	69	IT Solutions Inc	77
34	Global Consultants	128	70	Allied Informatics Inc	76
35	IBM	124	71	Ciber Inc	75
36	R Systems Inc	124	72	Deloitte Consulting LLC	75
37	Sprint United Mgt	124	73	Goldman Sachs	75
38	Wireless Facilities	124	74	Baton Rouge Intl	74
39	Cognizant Technology Solutions	123	75	Cyberthink	73
40	Satyam Computer Serv	123	76	Stanford University	73
41	Keane	114	77	Cap Gemini America	72
42	University of Washington	113	78	Infogain Corp	72
43	Analysts Intl Corp	110	79	Ajilon Serv	71
44	Capital One Serv	109	80	Allsoft Technologies Inc	71
45	Apar Infotech	108	81	Morgan Stanley Dean Witter	71
46	Modis Inc	108	82	Ericsson Inc	70
47	L & T Technology LTD	107	83	Harvard University	70
48	Complete Business Solutions Inc	105	84	Sabre Inc	70
49	Techspan	101	85	Yash Technologies Inc	70
50	CMOS Soft Inc	100	86	Pyramid Consulting Inc	69
51	Reniassance Worldwide	99	87	MSX Intl Inc	68
52	University of PA	97	88	Softplus Inc	67
53	Conexant Systems Inc	96	89	Baylor College Of Medicine	65
54	12 Technologies Inc	96	90	Microstrategy	65
55	AT T	93	91	University of Minnesota	65
56	Jean Martin	91	92	Universal Software	65
57	EMC	90	93	Computer Horizons	64
58	Atlantic Duncans Intl	87	94	Ramco Systems	63
59	Merrill Lynch	87	95	Siebel Systems Inc	63
60	Unique Computing	86	96	Insight Solutions Inc	62
61	Computer Intl	85	97	Synopsys Inc	62
62	Indotronix Intl	85	98	Texas Instruments Inc	62
63	Nationwide Insurance	84	99	Infosynergy	61
64	Interim Technology Consulting	84	100	Lason Systems Inc	61
65	Compaq Computer	80	101	Vanguard GR	61
66	GE	80	102	Yale University	61

Sub-total for 102 companies listed   13,940
Sub-total for companies not listed   67,322
Grand Total   81,262

These were just the top 100 companies listed on Form I-129, Petition for a Nonimmigrant Worker, within this timeframe. Counts represent a minimum number of approvals. In fact, there were thousands of companies submitting petitions. Some submitted multiple petitions with variations in spelling or abbreviations of the names so that petitions would appear to be submitted by different companies. Under the FOIA, I tried, and failed, to obtain current data. The DOL did, however, send me entire databases of H-1B information.

The next logical question seemed to be where are these workers coming from? Once again, the INS supplied that information.

Characteristics of Specialty Occupation Workers (H-1B)
May 1998 to July 1999
U.S. Immigration and Naturalization Service
February 2000
http://uscis.gov/graphics/shared/services/employerinfo/report1.pdf

Table reproduced from the above report.

| Country of Birth | Percent | | | Total |
	Estimate	95% Confidence Limits		
All Countries	100.0			134,400
India	47.5	(45.9	- 49.2)	63,900
China	9.3	(8.3	- 10.2)	12,400
United Kingdom	3.2	(2.6	- 3.8)	4,400
Canada	3.0	(2.4	- 3.5)	4,000
Philippines	2.7	(2.2	- 3.3)	3,700
Korea	2.3	(1.8	- 2.8)	3,100
Taiwan	2.1	(1.6	- 2.5)	2,800
Japan	2.0	(1.6	- 2.5)	2,700
Other countries	27.8	(26.4	- 29.3)	37,400

Clearly, these numbers would exceed the number of H-1B workers allowed in the U.S., but that is after adjustments and allowing for multiple petitions by some applicants and the fact that some petitions are revoked. Yet, even after the adjustments, the INS had to contract a private firm to assist in developing the final count, which appeared in the February 2000 report on the Characteristics of Specialty Occupation Workers (H-1B)— May 1998–July 1999.

The report also listed some other interesting information. From the same report, more than 83percent of the workers granted H-1B status were between the ages of 20 and34, approximately 53percent of the positions were for systems analysis or programming jobs, and all computer and engineering occupations accounted for 70percent of the total H-1B petitions, and nearly 74percent of the systems analysts and programmers were born in India compared to about 18percent in all other occupations.

Of the foreign workers between the ages of 20 and 34, 1,300 had only a high school diploma, 700 had associate degrees, and 1,100 either had no degree or the type of degree was unknown. Wait a minute, I thought that goal of H-1B petitions was to find people from other countries to fill U.S. jobs due to a lack of available people with the appropriate education and experience. Now we need to find people from other countries with high school and associates degrees to fill positions? One last thing bothering me about this report was that there were 1,100 unknown or none. We are letting people in the United States to fill positions and we don't even know what degree they have.

Again in 2002, the INS approved 197,537 H-1B petitions submitted by employers. Again, this exceeded the number allowed under the regulations.

U.S. Department of Homeland Security
Office of Immigration Statistics
Characteristics of Specialty Occupation Workers (H-1B): Fiscal Year 2002
Issued September 2003
Report Mandated by Public Law 105-277 Division C
American Competitive and Workforce Act of 1998
http://uscis.gov/graphics/shared/services/employerinfo/FY2002Charact.pdf

Table reproduced from this report

Below is the chart of H-1B Petitions Approved by Country of Birth of Beneficiary and Type of Petition: Fiscal Year 2002;

Country of birth	All Beneficiaries		Initial Employment		Continuing Employment	
	FY 2001 Number	FY2002 Number	FY 2001 Number	FY2002 Number	FY 2001 Number	FY2002 Number
Total	331,206	197,537	201,079	103,584	130,127	93,953
Country of birth known	330,521	197,092	200,627	103,350	129,894	93,742
India	161,561	64,980	90,668	21,066	70,893	43,914
China People's Republic	27,330	18,841	16,847	11,832	10,483	7,009
Canada	12,726	11,760	9,184	7,893	3,542	3,867
Philippines	10,389	9,285	7,294	6,648	3,095	2,647
United Kingdom	9,682	7,171	6,053	4,192	3,629	2,979
Korea	6,468	5,941	4,484	3,886	1,984	2,055
Japan	5,902	4,937	3,676	2,970	2,226	1,967
Taiwan	5,808	4,025	3,406	2,366	2,402	1,659
Pakistan	6,313	3,810	3,904	1,955	2,409	1,855
Columbia	3,703	3,320	2,909	2,362	794	958

Germany	4,205	3,291	2,598	1,955	1,607	1,336
France	4,151	3,145	2,748	1,925	1,403	1,220
Mexico	3,987	3,082	2,561	1,905	1,426	1,177
Russia	4,589	2,864	2,900	1,523	1,689	1,341
Venezuela	2,422	2,398	1,720	1,610	702	788
Brazil	2,900	2,287	1,947	1,414	953	873
Argentina	1,725	2,148	1,236	1,611	489	537
Turkey	2,292	2,004	1,517	1,319	775	685
Australia	2,273	1,846	1,487	1,107	786	739
Malaysia	2,532	1,771	1,464	900	1,068	871
Other countries	49,563	38,176	32,024	22,911	17,539	15,265
Country of birth unknown	685	445	452	234	233	211

This report from the Department of Homeland Security (DHS) shows the Country of Birth as unknown for many people entering into the U.S. Particularly in light of the events of 9/11, it would seem to be of paramount importance that people who cannot supply simple (and verifiable) information as to their place of birth should not be admitted to this country.

There are, of course, reports that are most favorably disposed toward the H-1B program and its impact on training for American workers.

United States General Accounting Office
Report to Ranking Minority Member, Subcommittee on Environment, Technology, and Standards, Committee on Science, House of Representatives
September 2003
H-1B Foreign Workers
Better Tracking Needed to Help Determine H-1B Program's Effects on U.S. Workforce
GAO-03-883

http://www.gao.gov/new.items/d03883.pdf

In this report, 36 of 145 H-1B employers agreed to speak with the Government Accounting Office (GAO), reporting that they had recruited, hired, and retained workers based on the skills needed, rather than the applicant's citizenship or Visa status. The percentage of H-1B employees who work for lower wages than their U.S. counterparts was, ostensibly, not known, at least not by these employers.

It is probably safe to assume that the H-1B workers (as well as the workers they displaced) know, however, even if they are unlikely to be asked. Other reports have shown that there is a substantial difference in salaries and that H-1B workers are often paid up to 30 percent less.

In this September 2003 report, the GAO states that The Department of Homeland Security (DHS) has incomplete information on H-1B worker entries, departures, and changes in visa status. The DHS cannot provide information on the number of H-1B workers in the United States at any time.

The citizens of the United States depend on federal agencies to keep track of the people who enter this country—to know where they are, where they came from, where they were born, why they are here, and whether they are here illegally. Yet as recently as September 2003, the DHS was unable to provide that information to the GAO. You can't blame the last guy in office for this one.

The report also stated that from March 2001 to March 2003 unemployment among highly educated individuals increased by 400,000, resulting in 1.2 million of these individuals being unemployed. In particular, employment substantially decreased within information technology (IT) occupations, for which employers often requested H-1B workers. With the tremendous amount of highly skilled workers being unemployed, companies still sought foreign help. Now, you can cry that you can't find help in a good economy, but companies were still seeking foreign workers even during this recession. Although, the demand was down for foreign workers, it was still there, in fact, booming.

Many employers stated that the process of getting H-1B workers could take anywhere between two to six months and that they paid an additional fee of $1,000 dollars to get premium processing. The processing costs and legal fees could result in an additional $2,500 to $8,000. In some cases certain fees could raise the cost up to $15,000. In the report, these employers also stated (presumably with straight faces) that H-1B status was not a factor in layoff decisions. Yet if an employer spends $15,000 dollars or more to get a worker into the United States, does it not stand to reason that the company will wish to protect that investment?

Of the 36 companies who agreed to provide information to the GAO, 31 stated that they would continue to use the H-1B process.

There have also instances in which H-1B workers who were unable to obtain residency were sent to the company's foreign office and then brought back on a new visa. This form of deception is permitted under the L-1 provision, which permits companies to use an intra-company transfer visa to bring in foreign professionals on a temporary basis. Because L-1 visas do not have an annual cap, companies may bring in as many workers as they desire. Moreover, these workers are not subject to prevailing U.S. wage laws. For the companies, the attraction of the L-1 provision is clear.

Little is known about the status of H-1B workers, even though the GAO report indicated that new systems are being developed. The DHS still cannot account for all the worker entries, departures, and other status changes using its current tracking systems.

We have all heard people in different professions complain of being overworked because of the lack of qualified workers in their field. Below is a partial list of some of the most common types of non-immigrant work visas. There are 24 major categories.

Nonimmigrant Work Visas

- H-1A   Nursing
- H-1B   Highly Skilled
- H-2A/H-2B   Agricultural/Temporary
- H-3   TemporaryTrainees
- B-1-/B-2   Business/Tourists
- E-1/E-2   Treaty trader/Treaty investor
- F-1/M-1/J   Student/Exchange visitor
- I   Press and Media
- TN   NAFTA
- L-1   Intra-company Transfers

Clearly, these visas cover almost every imaginable field—fields in which American workers, who may once have believed themselves to be indispensable, are now being replaced.

Chapter 2

Over $300 Million Dollars Given Out and Six Audits

The U.S. Office of the Inspector General (OIG) reports and audits on the H-1B programs make for fascinating reading, although if you want something to inspire confidence in your future as an American worker, these documents may not be the place to look. I don't mean to seem like a pessimist, but you don't need to come out with the happy-happy reports if you do one thing—hire Americans. Oh, and P.S. if things are so wonderful, why did you cancel the H-1B training program? I know why. We'll get to it, but before we do let's talk about the Office of the Inspector General (OIG).

One of my favorite departments in the U.S. Government is the Office of the Inspector General. You'll find the OIG everywhere, the Department of Labor, FBI, Homeland Security, so when I refer to the OIG, it depends on which federal agency I am covering. Many people think that this office only audits programs, but it also informs the Secretary, the Congress and the public sector whether programs are meeting expectations/goals.

It is important to look at the data and audits from the OIG reports regarding the H-1B program, because these are the people charged with the responsibility of honest reporting on programs.

When the OIG conducts an audit, their objective is to determine whether the grantee is meeting the intent of the H-1B Technical Skills Training Program and the requirements of the grant. The sub-objectives are to determine whether:

1. The project has been implemented as stated in the grant.
2. Program outcomes were measured, achieved, and reported.
3. Report outlays were reasonable, allocable, and allowable in accordance with Federal regulations, and the Office of Management and Budget Circular A-122, Cost Principals for Non-Profit Organizations.

The audits can be conducted during the course of the grant period. Because the findings of the audit can be appealed, the results are not final. Moreover, these findings do not include information on whether a company has reimbursed the DOL or whether DOL actually collected the funds.

I looked at several OIG audits of H-1B program grants awarded by the DOL to organizations for high-tech training programs to improve the technical skills of American workers. Organizations were allowed to respond to these audits, all of which are available on line along with responses to the same link. OIG also made some interesting recommendations, and organizations were given the opportunity to correct any problems before the grant period ended. Note: Remember, H-1B program training grants were awarded to organizations to help U.S. workers acquire technical skills, thus, presumably, obviating the need for the organization to import foreign workers to fill the same jobs. Also, multiple companies can participate in the same grant.

Audit of the Workplace, Inc.'s H-1B Technical Skills Training Grant Number AL-10854-00-60
March 27, 2000 To June 30, 2001
U.S. Department of Labor
Office of the Inspector General
Report No.: 02-02-207-03-390
Date: March 26, 2002

http://www.oig.dol.gov/cgi-bin/oa_rpts.cgi?s=h-1b&y=fy92002&a=03

Audit 1
Synopsis of the Audit

The first audit I examined was conducted at a firm called "The Workplace, Inc." OIG recommended the recovery of $140,000.

Grant to "The Workplace Inc." Received an H-1B Technical Skills Training designed to help U.S. acquire technical skills for occupations that are in demand and being filled by foreign workers. The Department of Labor awarded $1,500,000 for the period of March 27 2000–March 27, 2002. The Workplace is a nonprofit corporation that serves as a Workforce Investment Board for Fairfield County, Connecticut.

As of June 30, 2001 the OIG found that The Workplace, Inc. had not been successful in meeting the intent of the H-1B Technical Skills Training Program and the requirements of the grant.

- The Workplace paid $140,000 to Pepperidge Farm for Training. All of the training was for non-technical skills. The non-technical skills training courses at Pepperidge Farm were: diversity, diversity for leaders, presentation skills, basic selling, anti-harassment, interviewing, and coaching skills. Diversity or anti-harassment training made up 78 percent of training.
- Practically all of the classes were 2 to 4 hours in duration (with the exception of an 8 hour coaching skills course attended by 17 students). Seventy-nine percent of the participants attended only one class, and of those, 85 percent attended only anti-harassment or diversity training. These non-technical courses are of the type that any organization would provide to its employees. They were not

specific to H-1B occupations and should not be funded by this grant. In addition, no college credit was awarded for these courses.

- Pitney Bowes—The grant was designed to test skill transferability. However, the training given by Pitney Bowes, although in technical skills subjects, contained proprietary information, and therefore, was not intended to be shared with unemployed workers or individuals employed outside the company. Pitney Bowes was in the process of retooling for the manufacture of electronic rather than mechanical products, and it was necessary to train its workers in appropriate new skills, a training process that was in effect prior to the H-1B grant.
- Classes at Pitney Bowes varied from 4 to 60 hours and 89 percent of the participants attended only one class.
- Computronix—although Computronix is a participating H-1B company, it was not designated as a certified skills center, as was proposed for all H-1B companies. Information technology training was provided to Computronix employees at Norwalk Community College for $7,500. Training consisted of a 40-hour course.

The Workplace, Inc responses:

1. At the time of the audit, nine months remained in the grant award and an extension of the ending date had been requested
2. Changes had occurred in the regulations governing this program either during or right after the fieldwork completed, that were not reflected in the audit.
3. At the time the grant was written, the employees involved anticipated National Skills Standards be available. During the period in question, the National Skills Standards Board had not established standards thus reporting any outcome data relating to NSSB skills standards and/or certifications is not possible.
4. Corrective action had begun to remedy some discrepancies in the employer's billing, counting of participants and reporting on the Financial Status Report.

Based on the response to the draft report, we have eliminated the questioned administrative costs of $192,687. Subsequent to the end of the fieldwork, The Workplace and all other first round grantees, received grant modifications, which retroactively allowed administrative costs (not to exceed 10 percent of grant funds).

Audit of the New York Work Alliance H-1B Technical Skills Training Grant Number AH-10854-00-60
August 1, 2000 Through June 30, 2001
U.S. Department of Labor
Office of the Inspector General
Report No.: 02-02-211-03-390
Date: September 30, 2002

http://www.oig.dol.gov/cgi-bin/oa_rpts.cgi?s=h-1b&y=fy92002&a=03

Audit 2
Synopsis of Audit

The USDOL awarded the NY Work Alliance $2,940,162 for the period of August 1 2000–July 31 2002, to train 300 participants in information technology (IT) to meet demands for skilled workers in the Internet and DOT.COM industries.

As of June 30, 2001, the Work Alliance had not been successful in meeting the intent of the H-1B Technical Skills Training program and requirements of its grant. Most areas of the project were affected when demand for skilled workers in the Internet and DOT.COM industries declined significantly in (Cys) 2000 and 2001. Due to changes in the economy, the Work Alliance started to refocus the project by recruiting employers in other industries that needed IT workers. Nevertheless, the Work Alliance had not met essential grant requirements and the grant ending date is July 31, 2002.

1. The Work Alliance proposed and agreed to implement a project with three training tracks: web design and administration, employer-specific classroom training, and internships. Only one track and implemented, web design and administration. Employer-specific classroom training and internships had not yet been implemented. Additionally, as implemented, the project will not be sustainable after the grant expires.

2. The Work Alliance had not accomplished or accurately measured and reported program outcomes as stated in the grant. Training required by the grant was provided to only 40 percent of the participants (120 out of 300 participants). Placement outcomes were negligible with only two reported. Without related placements, the project does not meet the intent of the ACWIA technical skills training that participants be trained and placed in highly skilled H-1B occupations. The Work Alliance has a pending grant modification request to extend the grant period through January 31, 2003, to accomplish placements and upgrades.

3. We question $231,675, or 18 percent of Federal outlays, because these costs were not reasonable, allocable, or allowable. Further, the matching requirement of 25 percent was not being met as of June 30, 2001. Future costs may have to be questioned if the matching requirement is not met.

The Work Alliance's Response

In a response to our draft report, the President and Chief Operating Officer of the Work Alliance stated that he did not agree with the major conclusions of our report. He stated that the Work Alliance has continually sought to improve the program consistent with the intent of the grant solicitation, changing circumstances and feedback received from the USDOL.

OIG's Comments

Based on information submitted to the draft report, we have resolved classroom training costs of $64,800 that we had originally questioned. However, we have not changed our overall conclusion that as of June 30, 2001, the Work Alliance had not been successful in meeting the intent of the H-1B Technical Skills Training program and the requirements of the grant. Achieving placement outcomes is essential to the success of the H-1B Technical Training program and, as of June 30, 2001, the Work Alliance had achieved only two placements and had not implemented two of the three training tracks.

Recommendations

We recommend the Assistant Secretary for Employment and Training recover questioned costs of $231,675 and ensure that the Work Alliance operates the project in accordance with the intent and requirements of the grant.

Audit of the San Francisco Private Industry Council H-1B Technical Skills Training Grant Number AH-10855-00-60
August 1, 2000 Through December 31, 2001
U.S. Department of Labor
Office of the Inspector General
Report No.: 02-02-213-03-390
Date: September 30, 2002

http://www.oig.dol.gov/cgi-bin/oa_rpts.cgi?s=h-1b&y=fy92002&a=03

Audit 3
Synopsis of Audit

The USDOL awarded the San Francisco Private Industry Council (SFPIC) a technical skills training grant for the period August 1, 2000 through December 31, 2001. The findings of the audit were as follows.

1. The project had not been implemented as stated in the grant.
2. Program outcomes were measured, achieved, and reported
3. Reported costs were reasonable, allocable, and allowable in accordance with applicable Federal regulations, and Office of Management and Budget (OMB) Circular A-122, Cost Principals for Non-Profit Organizations.

The H-1B Technical Skills Training Program was designed to help U.S. workers acquire the technical skills for occupations that are in demand and being filled by foreign workers holding H-1B visas. USDOL awarded SFPIC $3,000,000 for the period of August 1, 2000 through July 31, 2002, to train and place up to 250 participants in digital media skill occupations.

Audit Results

As of December 31, 2001, SFPIC had implemented a sustainable training project that was consistent with grant requirements and server the target population. Reported costs totaled $1,885,057. However, SFPIC had not met planned placement outcomes and we question $915,985, or 49 percent of reported costs, that were not reasonable, allocable, and allowable.

1. While most training outcomes were achieved, planned placement outcomes did not occur due to decreased demand for digital media skill in the internet industry. The grant required SFPIC to report the number of participants placed into employment (placements), their average hourly wage (placements), and the number of participants remaining employed for at least 8 months after being hired (retention). SFPIC did not adequately measure retention outcomes. Also, SFPIC did not adequately measure retention outcomes. Also, SFPIC did not report placement wages or retention achievements to USDOL.

Program Outcome	Planned	Reported	Rate of Success
Placements	205	30	15%
Placement Wages	$22/hour	$15/hour	68%
Retention	200	Not reported	Unknown

2. We questioned $915,985 or 49 percent of reported costs of $1,885,057, because amounts claimed were not based on actual costs. Further, the matching requirement of 25 percent was not being met as of December 31, 2001. Future costs may be questioned if the matching requirement is not met.

SFPIC Response

On September 11, 2002, SFPIC's President responded to our draft report. She stated that she agreed that SFPIC had implemented a sustainable project consistent with the grant requirements but had not met planned placement outcomes as of December 31, 2001. She also provided additional documentation related to expenditures questioned in the draft report.

OIG Comments

The materials enclosed with SFPIC's response did not support cost of $915,985 and presented conflicting information from what had been obtained during the course of the audit.

Excerpts of the SFPIC's response to the draft report have been incorporated into appropriate sections of the report. The response is included in its entirety as an appendix.

Recommendations

We recommend that the Assistant Secretary for Employment and Training recover questioned costs of $915,985 and ensure that the SFPIC achieves planned placement outcomes, measures job retention, and fully reports program outcomes.

***

It is important to note that these outcomes are not final. Many of the findings have been contested, and in some instances, litigation is still pending. Also, a company may be able to prove that their costs were legitimate, and some decisions can be appealed.

There were other audits, and many of them were well performed.

The President's Fiscal Year (FY) 05 Budget Proposal provided some other interesting revelations.

http://www.whitehouse.gov/omb/budget/fy2005/labor.html

The Budget proposes the elimination of the H-1B Training Grants, which have not proven successful in raising the skills of U.S. workers in specialty occupations.

The Administration is now streamlining its permanent labor certification program to help employers who cannot find domestic workers to fill specialized occupations. Currently, applicants wait up to six years for permanent worker certifications. This has contributed to a backlog that now stands at over 300,000. The new process will help applicants by preventing backlogs while strengthening anti-fraud protections. DOL is also moving to eliminate significant backlogs in employer applications filed under the old process. The Budget also proposes a new permanent program application fee to finance the cost of processing new applications and partially support backlog reduction in state and regional offices.

It is reasonable to ask what happens to all of those federal workers who worked on a program that has "not been proven successful in raising the skills of U.S. workers in specialty occupations." Will they be retrained, or should we go outside the U.S. to find replacements for the people who worked on the H-1B grant program?

Over $300,000 million was invested in the federal; H-1B program, granted not from taxpayers dollars, but from the loss of potential income generated by American workers. There should be some accountability. If a similar situation occurred in the private sector, i.e., several hundred million dollars was spent on a training program that did not achieve the intended goals, I think it is safe to say that heads would roll.

In retrospect, taxpayers are entitled to an explanation as to why the failure of the H-1B program could not have been recognized several million dollars earlier. Yet it would appear that no such explanation is forthcoming.

Worse, however, is that the H-1B program had great potential. Had the program been successful, thousands of American workers could have been trained and remained competitive. Indeed, H-1B could have been one of the finest federal programs ever adopted. Instead, it was a $300 million boondoggle, mismanaged by the government and abused by corporations almost from the beginning.

Will there ever be an investigation to determine what exactly went wrong? Maybe, but I was unable to find evidence of any such investigation, thus far.

Perhaps, as I said at the outset, the H-1B program was just an excellent example of The Law of Unintended Consequences.

In any case, corporations and organizations that still claim to be unable to find enough highly skilled workers should find relief in the President's FY 05 Budget Proposal. What this will mean for American workers remains to be seen.

Chapter 3

I'll Get Back to You in Eight Months!

If you had trouble starting your car on a cold day, would you wait 240 days to fix it? If you were the DOL, you might.

Office of the Inspector General
Evaluation of the Audit Resolution Process
Report No. 2E-03-001-0001
Date Issued: March 5, 2002"

http://www.oig.dol.gov/public/reports/oace/fy2002/2e030010001.PDF

This report deals with the efficiency and effectiveness of the DOL audit resolution process. Although one would think that fixing the problems identified should be part of any successful audit that is not always the case.

Finding A

In this report, the OIG found that audit findings and recommendation are not being resolved within the 180-day regulatory time limit. Of 41 reports sampled, issues had been resolved for only 14. The average resolution time was approximately 240 days for OIG and DOL agency management. OIG believes that the major reason for this delay is that neither agency is following established procedures. For example:

1. DOL agency management is not enforcing the 180-day time limit.
2. Auditees are not as responsive as they should be.
3. Many times, there are complex issues that require additional research.
4. Issues need to be coordinated within the respective agency and with outside agencies such as OIG and DOL

Recommendations

1. OIG provide audit staff with guidance and training on procedures for resolving audit findings
2. DOL agency management provide guidance and training to staff on procedures for resolving audit findings
3. OIG implement procedures requiring that, once an issue has been identified during the audit fieldwork, auditors should contact DOL agency management

to get their insight and input for consideration as recommendations for corrective action

4. DOL agency management develop procedures including steps for providing insight and input to auditors regarding issues that identified during the audit process.

5. OIG implement procedures to provide auditees with incentives and opportunities throughout the audit process to locate and provide any requested documentation. For example, whenever documentation is not provided, the auditors should contact the Grant or Contract Officer to solicit assistance in obtaining the requested documentation

6. DOL agency management implement procedures that allow for OIG auditors to review any documentation submitted by auditees during the course of resolution

7. DOL agency management explore the benefits/ramifications of implementing punitive measures for grantees and contractors who do not provide documentation to auditors during the audit process.

Corrective action

1, 2, 4, 5, 6 and 7 resolved. 3 not resolved

Go back and re-read item 5. "OIG implement procedures to provide auditees with incentives and opportunities throughout the audit process to locate and provide any requested documentation." Is it not reasonable to assume that receiving millions of dollars in grants, i.e., money that does not have to be repaid, should be sufficient incentive for cooperating with auditors? One might also ask why no consideration was apparently given to training OIG staff in established audit procedures before these sizeable grants were made?

Finding B

Steps that can be taken to improve the audit process:

1. Communication between OIG auditors and DOL agency management can be improved.

2. OIG auditors should take extra steps to obtain documentation prior to questioning costs due to lack of documentation.

The DOL has been administering grants for many years. Is it reasonable to assume that these problems have only come to light recently?

This report came out in March of 2002. About a year and a half later, the H-1B program was cancelled. The loss of this program represents a tremendous loss of opportunity for the American worker, especially for those whose careers were cut short due to lack of training in necessary skills. The oversight and survival of this program should have been a top priority. That grant recipients should have been more closely monitored is blatantly obvious. Quarterly audits of DOL practices and procedures would have helped to ensure more efficient grant management as well. It is a frightening question, but what if the people responsible for handling this grant program are simply reassigned to a different grant program without any additional oversight or training to prevent similar egregious errors?

There have been assurances that efforts are underway to resolve some of the problems that eventually sunk the H-1B program. As taxpayers and, more important, as American workers, we can only hope that these efforts do not turn out to be too little, and too late to head off a similarly costly reoccurrence.

This OIG report speaks for itself, not only about the DOL, but also about the OIG itself.

Chapter 4

Outsourcing—The Next Best Thing to Bringing Them Here

Outsourcing has become yet another solution to finding cheap labor.

By simply setting up a facility overseas, almost any company can pay a mere 10 percent in labor costs for a foreign worker to perform the same job as an American worker. In short, the company can realize considerable savings by having to pay a foreign worker only 10 percent of what they pay you. Factor in the absence of health care, unions, and federal regulations that govern U.S. businesses, and the savings become enormous. The mere thought is enough to make any American CEO salivate. Of course, outsourcing has its problems, but for a 90 percent cost savings, companies are willing to endure an awful lot.

Think about the savings in terms of health care costs alone.

Every time you go to a doctor, a clinic, or a hospital somebody is taking notes. When you have any type of procedure done in a hospital, there has to be a record. The doctor will dictate notes on your procedure, the condition, and whatever other information he or she deems to be relevant. Your medical records are then sent out for transcription and review before they are returned to the doctor. Transcriptionists are paid, on average, about 8 or 9 cents per line for these reports. That may not sound like much, until you consider that many transcriptionists can do 3,000 to 4,000 lines per day. A good transcriptionist can earn $60K per year. Of course, transcriptionists must be bonded. They are held responsible for the material on which they work, thus their careers depend on their ability to maintain the patient's privacy. Medical data is one of the last forms of information that is still comparatively difficult to access.

For years medical transcriptionists were almost exclusively American workers. Then it dawned on the companies that, whereas here they had to pay 8 or 9 cents per line, in places such as India, Israel, or Russia, the cost dropped to 3 cents per line, not counting the extra savings in not having to provide additional benefits. Three cents a line may not constitute a living wage in this country, but in other countries it is a veritable fortune.

The initial results from outsourcing this work were not good, in part because of the language barriers. Over time, however, there was a dramatic improvement in the quality of the outsourced work. Today, the transcribed records done overseas are returned very close to perfect.

Transcription is a multi-billion dollar industry that is changing by the minute. In addition to lower wages and no overhead costs, networking and the Internet have made outsourcing more and more attractive. As technology continues to improve, the cost of doing business abroad will decrease even further. Soon, American transcription companies, with American workers, will no longer be able to compete.

If you think this is the only type of medical information work that is being outsourced, think again. What if you had an MRI that was sent overseas to be read by a physician in another country and the results then sent back here? This is no longer a hypothetical question. It is already being done, and has been ongoing for some time.

Part of the problem with sub-contracted medical work is loss of control over where the information is and where it has been. The consequences can be devastating.

San Francisco Chronicle, March 28, 2004 by David Lazarus
http://sfgate.com/cgi-bin/article.cgi?file=/c/a/2004/03/28/MNGFS3080R264.DTL

To read the entire article please use the link provided.

Lubna Baloch sat in her office in the sprawling Pakistani commercial center of Karachi and gazed at the e-mail she'd composed. She tried to imagine the reaction half a world away when the people at UC San Francisco Medical Center saw what she'd written.

The famous U.S. hospital would have to take her seriously, Baloch knew, when it realized she was prepared to post its confidential patient records on the Internet. That is, unless UCSF helped her get the money she was owed from the mysterious Tom Spires, her link in a long chain of medical transcription subcontractors.

"Your patient records are out in the open to be exposed," Baloch wrote in her e-mail, "so you better track that person and make him pay my dues or otherwise I will expose all the voice files and patient records of UCSF Parnassus and Mt. Zion campuses on the Internet."

Then the kicker: "Just to make you believe that I am not bluffing I am attaching latest voice file and text of your hospital." Baloch had included private discharge summaries for two UCSF patients.

She clicked the send button on her computer screen.

The message arrived at UCSF on Oct. 7, 2003. It would get a swift reaction from hospital officials, but not in the way Baloch was expecting. Her brief e-mail would send shock waves throughout the U.S. medical establishment and prompt legislation to change California privacy laws. People's livelihoods, including her own, would be ruined.

"This was an egregious breach," said Tomi Ryba, chief operating officer of UCSF Medical Center, adding that what happened to her hospital could happen to any company that outsources data. "We'll have to live with this risk on a daily basis."

American jobs have been moving offshore for years, primarily manufacturing work seeking out lower-paid workers abroad. The outsourcing of people's personal information, though, is a relatively new phenomenon—opening the door to identity theft, fraud and other criminal activities.

"We've reached the point where American companies ship personal information outside the country and tell customers to check their privacy at the shore," said Rep. Edward Markey, D-Mass., one of the leading privacy advocates on Capitol Hill.

Lubna Baloch's run-in with UCSF demonstrates that the safety of outsourced information can never be guaranteed—no matter how stringent the safeguards—and offers the most glaring example to date of how a disgruntled overseas worker can violate the privacy rights of U.S. citizens.

The UC San Francisco medical center had never contracted with this Pakistani woman directly One can only guess at the shock and horror experienced by the medical center upon receiving this threatening email from someone they knew nothing whatsoever about. They had done nothing wrong, nothing different than what had been done for years.

This could have happened anywhere to anyone.

Many hospitals contract their work out, but it usually ends with one or two subcontractors. In this case, the patient records made their way half way around the world to someone who expected to be paid immediately.

In a different professional vein, a friend of mine went to the unemployment office recently where he met seven people whose computer programming jobs had been outsourced to India. My research revealed that the company that had outsourced the jobs had also only recently received a grant—an H-1B grant—to train American workers to help them become more competitive.

How much is enough? Companies posting record profits are still looking for ways to increase the bottom line. It never seems to occur to them that putting those efforts behind ways to enhance the professional growth of their employees would mean even greater increases in profits.

Something is going to break. You may see a shift back toward unions—for office workers, high tech workers, and dozens of other positions for which unions were never considered. This is what may be necessary to redress a terrible balance.

All over the U.S. seminars are being conducted to show companies how to outsource, what to outsource, what will happen to the business if they do not outsource, and hundreds of creative outsourcing methods. The big winners will be stockholders, attorneys, outsourcing trainers, and politicians, among many others.

The big losers will be the United States and the American worker.

Below is a short course of instruction I created on the real meaning of outsourcing terminology. You may want to jot this down for future reference.

Phrase	Meaning
Outsourcing is good for the economy.	Corporations are contributing big bucks to my campaign.
Outsourcing creates jobs.	It's creating jobs for everybody except Americans.
Outsourcing helps our economy grow.	I was able to fire all my workers and hire people who for 90 percent less.
Outsourcing creates change.	I do not have to pay them benefits.
Outsourcing solves many problems that cannot be solved here.	I do not have to deal with anybody (especially those unions.)
We outsource only because we cannot find skilled labor (like H-1Bs).	I do not have to pay a fee to get somebody here, and I still save tons of money.
Outsourcing will help expand our business.	The stockholders will love it when I post 2 cents a share above projected earnings. Who cares about screwing a family out of a job, after all I am the CEO.
We only outsource for certain jobs that cannot be performed here. Well, you get it.	I would outsource the janitor if I could figure a way to do it.

We know that there are dangers involved in outsourcing, but companies are willing to take the risk because of the tremendous cost savings and because outsourcing allows them to avoid all the headaches involved with unions, benefits (particularly health care), overhead, etc.

There is a dangerous myth making the round, which says that only computer jobs can be outsourced. The unemployment lines are full of people who were in accounting, customer service, help desk support, tax preparation, payroll, manufacturing, construction, engineering, and a host of other positions, who believed that myth right up until their jobs got sent overseas.

Suppose, rather than pay you $30 an hour, your company decides t outsource your job, have the work prefabricated overseas, and then do the final assembly here? That's just one of many possible (likely?) scenarios.

Clearly, there are still certain jobs that cannot be outsourced, but the ball is in play and new outsourcing possibilities are in high demand.

Of course, one cannot discuss this issue without noting that this is an election year and, as usual, candidates are collecting hundreds of millions of dollars in campaign contributions. This year, especially, we are likely to see a decline in the H-1B numbers and a corresponding increase in the national rate of employment. Tangentially, there will be a lot of talk about how "jobs have been created." Yet, every career politician (regardless of party) knows that one of the smartest things to do in a election year is to cut back on immigration so that American companies (briefly) have no choice but to hire American workers.

What happens after the election? Will the drumbeat about the "shortage of skilled workers" be heard around the country again, closely followed by the sound of American workers being tossed overboard in favor of cheaper, foreign workers?

As is so happens, there is a shortage of skilled trade labor. Construction workers, equipment operators, carpenters, ironworkers, cement masons, bricklayers, truck drivers, etc. Look no further than recent history to see how this problem will be solved. Where there are job shortages, there will be H-1B workers, going by another name perhaps, but still ready to fill the positions left by "unskilled" American workers.

Remember the "shortage of skilled computer workers"? That was solved by the importation of approximately one million workers almost all of whom came with computer skills. Presto! No more shortage.

Is there any reason to believe that, after the election, the problem shortage of skilled trade workers will not be similarly "solved"?

I think not.

Chapter 5
The Shortage That Didn't Exist

United States General Accounting Office
Report to Congressional Requesters
March 1998
Information Technology
Assessment of the Department of Commerce's Report on Workforce Demand
GAO/HEHS-98-106

http://www.gao.gov/archive/1998/he98106.pdf

In a 1998 report to Congress, the GAO raised questions about the so-called shortage of Information Technology (IT) workers. Based on projections from the Commerce Department Bureau of Labor Standards (BLS), the report concluded that there would be a demand for slightly over one million additional IT workers.

BLS projections for new IT workers over the 11 years between 1994 to 2005 include IT workers to fill newly created jobs (820,000) in the three IT occupational categories (computer programmers, systems analysts, and computer scientists/engineers) and to replace workers (227,000) who are leaving these fields as a result of retirement, change of profession, or other reasons.

The report noted that projected job growth for all occupations between 1994 and 2005 is 14 percent. Since the report was issued, Commerce has issued an update with revised BLS projections showing an even stronger growth. The new figures showed 1.3 million projected job openings between 1996 and 2006 with ~1.1 million of these jobs due to growth alone.

The report from the GAO stated that the Commerce Department analysis of the supply of IT workers did not consider the following

- Numerical data for degrees and certifications in computer and information sciences other than at the bachelor's level when they quantify the total available supply;
- College graduates with degrees in other areas;
- Workers who have been, or will be, retrained for these occupations.

According to the GAO report, the Commerce Department also stated that India now has more than 200,000 programmers and that, in conjunction with U.S. corporate partners, has now become the world's largest exporter of software. In 1996 and 1997, outsourced software development accounted for 41 percent of India's software exports. Commerce also cited a report indicating that companies are searching for IT workers in foreign labor markets.

The Commerce report identified the decline in the number of computer science graduates as a factor contributing to an inadequate supply of IT workers.

The GAO reported that Commerce's report has serious analytical and methodological weaknesses that undermine the credibility of its conclusion that a shortage of IT workers exists.

In its defense, the Commerce Department stated that its report was never intended to be definitive, exhaustive analysis of the IT labor market. Rather the report was an initial effort to explore a *potential* shortage of IT workers. The Acting Under Secretary stated that the GAO had mischaracterized the Commerce Department report, and that in fact the report did not corroborate an existing shortage of IT workers.

Even assuming that the Acting Under Secretary was right, the kinds of numbers that appeared in the Commerce Department report were open to great deal of largely self-serving interpretation. To state that "X" number of workers will be needed during a certain period, while only "Y" number of qualified graduates will be available, is an open invitation for any company to argue in favor of the importation of foreign workers.

The GAO report came out in 1998 just prior to a recession and increase in H-1B immigration to 195,000 workers per year. Had immigration levels not been increased, the impact on the IT field would have been far less devastating.

Even during a recession, there is often a frenzied demand for more foreign workers. This is because, with the exception of American workers, everyone benefits from this importation.

The question remains: Was there actually a shortage of IT workers or did the Commerce Department report merely reinforce industry arguments for the need for foreign workers?

India's outsourced software development accounted for 41 percent of the country's software exports. Numbers that high indicate that a country is well on its way to dominating a field—in this case IT.

Between 2000 and 2004, the country was experiencing a massive recession as a result of which millions of Americans were (are?) aggressively looking for work. At that same time, 195,000 foreign workers per year were being brought into the country. In other words, during a recession, with millions of American workers looking for jobs, American companies imported approximately 800,000 foreign workers. Remember, these numbers do not take into account the amount of outsourcing and off-shoring taking place at the same time.

Add to this the complicated and often misleading figures on overall unemployment.

THE EMPLOYMENT SITUATION: JUNE 2004

http://www.bls.gov/news.release/empsit.nr0.htm

In a BLS report, it was stated that non-farm payroll continued to rise in June, and the unemployment rate remained at 5.6percent.

"Both the unemployment rate, 5.6 percent, and the number of unemployed persons, 8.2 million, were essentially unchanged in June. The unemployment rate has been 5.6 in all but one month this year."

Below is a list of the employment rates from paragraph 2.

Adult men	5.0 percent
Adult women	5.0 percent
Teenagers	16.8 percent
Whites	5.0 percent
Blacks	10.1 percent
Hispanics or Latinos	6.7 percent

The report went on to state:

"The number of persons who were marginally attached to the labor force was 1.5 million in June, about the same as a year earlier. (Data are not seasonally adjusted.) These individuals wanted and were available to work and had looked for a job sometime in the prior 12 months."

The report also notes that there were 478,000 discouraged workers. Discouraged workers are a subset of the marginally attached, in that they believed there was no work for them.

The BLS report estimates that there were 8.2 million unemployed workers during the time period covered. Conveniently, perhaps, this does not include the approximately half million people who are so discouraged that they have given up looking for work.

Again, according to the BLS report, in June there were job gains in health care and social assistance, professional and technical services, and transportation and warehousing. Manufacturing employment edged lower following several months of small increases, and construction employment was flat.

Before one accepts all this information as factual, it might be useful to look at how the government actually defines employment vs. unemployment.

How the Government Measures Unemployment

http://www.bls.gov/cps/cps_htgm.htm

What are the basic concepts of employment and unemployment?

The basic concepts involved in identifying the employed and unemployed are simple:

- People with jobs are *employed.*
- People who are jobless, looking for jobs, and available for work are *unemployed.*
- People who are neither employed nor *unemployed are not in the labor force.*

Who is counted as employed?

"Not all of the wide range of job situations in the American economy fit neatly into a given category. For example, people are considered employed if they did any work at all for pay or profit during the survey week. This includes all part-time and temporary work, as well as regular full-time year-round employment".

Who is counted as unemployed?

"Persons are classified as unemployed if they do not have a job, have actively looked for work in the prior 4 weeks, and are currently available for work".

In other words, people who want work, but who have not "actively looked" for work in the 4 weeks prior to the survey, are not considered "unemployed."

Finally, and perhaps because intangibles are difficult to assess in statistical terms (even if the assessment is inherently flawed), one wonders how many people have accepted huge decreases in salary, taken second (even third) jobs just to have health care, or sold their homes when unemployment benefits ran out.

Proving, once again, that real life and statistics are two different animals.

Chapter 6
Visas—The Security of a Nation

The information I obtained for this chapter was, in many ways, the most frightening. The link between immigration visas and terrorism is a real and present danger to this country. Yet, for all the resources that are being poured into Homeland Security, remarkably little is being done to address this crucial problem.

It is important to note from the beginning that many people want to gain access to the United States for perfectly legitimate reasons including business, travel, and even employment.

Access to this country, as to most other countries, is gained through the issuance of a visa. Controlling, monitoring, and tracking the people to whom visas are issued should be, but alas is not, a top priority. Suffice to say almost all of the terrorists responsible for the 9/11 attacks were here on visas issued by our government.

The pressure from companies hungry for foreign labor to increase the number of visas issued is relentless. Are we compromising the security of our nation for higher corporate profits?

Since 9/11, there have been (we are told) tremendous improvements in securing our borders and numerous other steps have been taken to enhance our safety and preparedness in the event of another attack. We have spent tens of millions of dollars on new facilities, new computer systems and databases to flag, track, and stop potential terrorists. How well prepared are we?

Below is an excerpt from a document archived in the Department of Justice (DOJ).

In The United States District Court For The Eastern District Of Virginia
Alexandria Division
"(Proposed Redacted) Affidavit In Support Of Application For Search Warrant (October 2003)

http://www.usdoj.gov/usao/vae/ArchivePress/OctoberPDFArchive/03/safaaffid102003.pdf

In an Affidavit in Support of a Search Warrant, it describes several individuals in the United States who were here on visas.

The acronym PIJ (Palestine Islamic Jihad-Shikaki Fraction)—SDT Speciality Designated Terrorists, also known as the Islamic Jihad of Palestine. Described as terrorists organizations dedicated to the elimination of the State of Israel.

In #21 of the affidavit, "Ramadan Abdullah Shallah is described as the current leader of the PIJ and resides in Damascus, Syria. An SDT, Shallah replaced PIJ founder Fathi Shikaki as the leader of the PIJ, after Shikaki's assassination in Malta in 1995. Prior to taking this position, Shallah had resided in Tampa, Florida.

Jihad is a holy war aimed at killing every enemy of Islam, including (among others) the New World Order symbolized by the United States. Shallah stated that Muslims should not be defensive or apologize against charges of terrorism, because Jihad required them to terrorize, devastate, humiliate, and degrade their enemies.

This was a professor at the University of Florida on an (H-1B). Although this is an incident that seems to stick out because Ramadan Abdullah Shallah took over as leader of the PIJ, this is only one of the many visa holders who are in the US with ulterior motives. P.S. The indictment came in October 2003. Eight years after he left!

This is only one of the many cases in which terror cells operate in the U.S. Many of these people come into the U.S. on visas and live and work in the community while their ultimate goal is destruction.

Shallah was a temporary specialized worker. He also had three different visas filed on his behalf.

I understand that people who enter the U.S. under a visa and are involved in terror may be a small amount. Then again, nobody knows. So we should be using every tool we have at our fingertips to ensure that everyone entering the United States, especially on a long-term work visa, is here for legitimate reasons.

I often heard that the FBI has shifted many agents onto the job of tracking down terrorists, but they are understaffed. I hear all the terrorist alerts that are issued every week and it is almost like it's expected to hear about a new threat.

The problem I have with all this is that this visa system is being neglected, and has been for a long time.

An Investigation Regarding the Removal of a Tiffany Globe from the Fresh Kills Recovery Site
December 2003
Office of the Inspector General
http://www.usdoj.gov/oig/special/0403a/index.htm

This report describes an investigation based on an allegation that an FBI special agent removed a Tiffany and Co. crystal globe paperweight from the Fresh Kills Landfill, which served as the World Trade Center recovery site and gave it to an FBI secretary. The agent was part of an Evidence response team deployed to New York City following the 9/11 attacks.

"This matter was presented to the United States Attorney's Office for the Southern District of New York, which declined prosecution of the removal of the globe from the Fresh Kills recovery site."

Executive Assistant Director told the OIG that "since he was the Inspector in charge for the PENTTBOMB investigation, in the late fall of 2001 he requested pieces of the WTC building from [**REDACTED**] for himself and possibly others working on the investigation. He said he asked for a piece of the building as memento, and advised that FBI personnel had taken non-evidentiary items from prior terrorist incident sites as mementos. He said he did not receive a piece of the building from [**REDACTED**] until June 2003. He denied asking for items from dignitaries or giving any WTC debris items to dignitaries."

"All members of the Minneapolis ERT described the management at both Ground Zero and Fresh Kills as chaotic and unorganized. They said there was no real chain of command at either site, and no one knew who was in charge. They said they would be told one thing one day, and then told something entirely different the next."

"FBI personnel who removed items from Fresh Kills gave several different justifications for doing so, including:

- Fresh Kills was not a crime scene
- The items were non-evidentiary and of no value
- Other federal, state, and local agencies were removing items
- They were given authorization
- There was FBI precedent for taking items"

"Also, with regard to FBI employees claiming they could take items of no value, it should be noted that items from the debris, even pieces of the building, could be considered historic memorabilia or artifacts, making them items of value. As mentioned earlier, the United States Attorney's Office in Minneapolis had considered charging a civilian with removing a fire truck door that curators estimated, as a WTC artifact, had a value exceeding $5,000. As also previously noted, a sculpture made from the debris, which was given at no cost to family members of the victims, recently sold on eBay for $255."

"Our investigation revealed that the removal of items as mementos and for display purposes by FBI personnel did not only occur at the WTC recovery sites. Several FBI personnel interviewed in this case justified taking mementos based on FBI precedent. As previously mentioned one ERT member stated he "saw the taking of mementos as an accepted common practice throughout the FBI." Interviews revealed that non-evidentiary items had been removed as mementos from previous crime scenes pertaining:

- The U.S. Embassy Bombings in Africa (1998)", here building pieces, a U.S. flag, and an African bunting were taken by FBI personnel.
- The Execution of a Search Warrant at the Cabin of Convicted Unabomber Ted Kaczynski (1996) where elk antlers and shingles and other pieces of the cabin were taken by FBI personnel
- The Bombing of the Alfred J. Murrah Federal Building in Oklahoma City (1995), where building pieces were taken by FBI personnel and engraved with the FBI seal and the date of tragedy

Some NY ERT members also told the OIG that had they seen non-evidentiary building pieces from the Bombing of Khobar Towers in Saudi Arabia (1996), and the WTC Bombing (1993) in the possession of other FBI employees. Yet, we have no indication that any item worth the value of the Tiffany globe was removed from any of these sites."

The Federal Bureau of Investigation's Efforts to Improve the Sharing of Intelligence and Other Information
U.S. Department of Justice, Office of the Inspector General Audit Division
Audit Report 04-10
December 2003
http://www.justice.gov/oig/audit/FBI/0410/final.pdf

In a report that is redacted and unclassified, the OIG reported the following;

Page i
"The Federal Bureau of Investigation (FBI) has established as its highest priority the prevention of terrorists attacks on the United States. The accomplishment of this critical national security mission requires the FBI to collect, analyze, and appropriately disseminate intelligence and other activities. However, in the past, Congressional inquiries concerning the September 11, 2001, terrorists attacks on the United States, reports of commissions examining terrorism before and since September 11, and Office of the Inspector General (OIG) reports have suggested various weaknesses in the FBI'S ability to effectively carry out the vital intelligence component of its counterterrorism program."

Page ii
"The terrorist attacks of September 11, 2001, revealed severe deficiencies in the FBI's intelligence analysis and information-sharing capabilities and processes. During the OIG's September 2002 Audit of the FBI's counterterrorism program, some FBI managers described the FBI's intelligence analysis capability as "broken." Other on terrorism-related commissions and in Congress have suggested that the FBI's intelligence capability was more than broken; it had been virtually non-existent".

SALE—Buy one visa get a green card free!

OIG
U.S. Department of State and the Broadcasting Board of Governors

Office of the Inspector General
Case Number 02-022

http://oig.state.gov/oig/inv/summaries/visa/14417.htm

An OIG investigator received information from the U.S. Border Patrol that the laser visas being issued to Mexican nationals did not qualify to receive them. You can't qualify for many reasons, especially if you are a criminal or if you have been deported or if you have been a bad, bad, boy.

Except that five of the new and improved laser visas did not actually match the fingerprints to the person that the visa was issued to.

When the OIG traveled to the consulate in January 2002, with the help of RSO and USBP agent, they conducted a series of reviews and interviews. They found that two FSNs employed at the consulate had been issuing laser visas to Mexican nationals.

The two were paid $1,000 for each visa and had issued five or six off-site during each trip.

There were also two other FSNs who worked for the consulate that had engaged in similar activity.

All four were terminated from employment.

Well, there is always an argument that this was an isolated incident and that things like this just don't happen every day. True, they don't. When you spend tens of millions of dollars to develop these systems, there is always the chance of an isolated incident. Take for example the isolated incident below:

Former U.S. Embassy Employees Plead Guilty to Visa Fraud
Husband-wife team will serve minimum of five years in prison

http://usinfo.state.gov/gi/Archive/2004/May/03-527337.html

On April 30, 2004 two former employees of the U.S. Embassy in Colombo, Sri Lanka, pleaded guilty to charges relating to a large-scale visa fraud ring. The term large scale makes me reach for the aspirin bottle.

Apparently, a husband and wife team accepted large sums of money from people in California and other places for issuing visas to the United States of America. The people were from Vietnam, India and other countries.

This scheme included visa fraud, bribery of public officials, and honest services wire fraud. This operation involved the payment of hundred of thousands of dollars by people in exchange for the issuance of visas to foreign nationals.

No matter what system you put into place, you have to realize that the control of every visa is critical or nothing works. We are only one terrorist away from another 9/11 catastrophe.

The Visa Diversity Program encourages emigration from countries that are not well represented in this country. These countries include Cuba, Syria, Libya, and Iran. Many of the countries whose citizens are encouraged to emigrate have been identified as countries that sponsor terrorists.

Again, the OIG appears to be the only federal agency that is attempting to rectify these situations. If their success with the DOL is any indication, there is every reason to be worried. Very worried.

State Department Finds Security Risk in Diversity Visa Law
Recommends Congress ban applicants from terrorism-sponsoring nations
http://usinfo.state.gov/gi/Archive/2004/Apr/30-890489.html

The OIG of the U.S. State Department has found that the Visa Diversity Program might open the door to terrorists or agents of hostile governments. Their April 29th report to Congress suggests changes be made.

Hearing testimony from all witnesses is available at

http://www.house.gov/judiciary/immigration.htm

Here's a report that will make you sleep better at night knowing that after all the problems we had in this country will terrorism and visas, we seem to correct the problems and we can move on.

U.S. Department of Energy
Office of Inspector General
Office of Audit Services
Audit Report, The Departments Unclassified Foreign Visits and Assignments
DOE/IG-0579, December 2002

http://www.ig.doe.gov/pdf/ig-0579.pdf

When the audit was conducted, there were two separate laboratories that had been mentioned. Two separate offices, managed by the Office of Science (Science) and the National Nuclear Security Administration (NNSA) permitted foreign nationals to access their facilities without ensuring that the visitors or assignees had properly admitted or were authorized to remain in the United States.

The Science-managed laboratory also granted visitors and assignees site access before official approval and, in many cases before the National Security Agency (NSA) background checks or consultations with counterintelligence.

Information is supposed to be maintained on each foreign national visitor and assignee. The visa is important because it establishes the status of the foreign national's status, such as student, diplomat, or government official.

Neither of these labs required or maintained accurate passport and visa information for 91 of the 187 (49 percent) randomly selected visitors or assignees. Forty-one had active badges and could have accessed most of the site's facilities. Thirty-four of the 91 were from sensitive countries such as the People's Republic of China, India, and Russia. There were similar problems at the other lab NNSA-managed. Thirty-seven of 188 (randomly sampled) had passport data and visa data that was missing or incomplete. At the time, twelve had active badges, 17 were from sensitive countries.

Many of the assignees from sensitive countries were allowed site access before their background checks or counterintelligence consultations were completed. One of these individuals was from Iran, a country identified by the U.S. Department of State as a terrorist supporting country, and was allowed site access over two months before the background check was completed.

Here's my favorite part of this, "To its credit, the Department has taken a number of actions to improve accountability of its foreign visits and assignments program. During the course of the audit, the Office of Security issued a draft directive on policy and procedures for managing unclassified foreign national access to Department facilities for comment. This directive, if ultimately adopted and implemented, should address a number of our recommendations."

I think the part that bothers me the most is that this was after 9/11. By not following the process, you are putting every person in this country at risk.

United States Embassy
Tokyo, Japan
7 Nations Cited as Sponsors of Terror in State Department Report
Iran remain most active state sponsor, U.S. report says

http://japan.usembassy.gov/e/p/tp-20030501b2.html

"The seven designated state sponsors of terrorism did not take the necessary steps in 2002 to disassociate themselves fully from their ties to terrorism, according to the Department of State's annual international terrorism report.

The "Patterns of Global Terrorism: 2002" report, released April 30, identifies Cuba, Iran, Iraq, Libya, North Korea, Syria, and Sudan as state sponsors of terrorism."

Now Iran was listed as one of the most active sponsors of terrorism, but we still are allowing foreign visits to our national laboratories. It makes me a little nervous thinking that our labs are open. Maybe, I should explain why this seems to bother me more than I would even like to think about.

Probably one of the most important points of this book involving the security of the United States was something I found introduced in the Senate. It bothered me so much that I felt I had to include it in its entirety. It is lengthy; however after reading it you will understand why I included it.

S.666
Biological, Chemical, and Radiological Weapons Countermeasures Research Act
(Introduced in Senate)
March 19, 2003

http://thomas.loc.gov/cgi-bin/query/D?c108:1:./temp/~c108N7cZtS:
When searching—http://thomas.loc.gov enter the Word/Phrase—"Biological, Chemical, and Radiological Weapons Countermeasures Research Act"

S.666
Biological, Chemical, and Radiological Weapons Countermeasures Research Act
(Introduced in Senate)

SECTION 1. SHORT TITLE; TABLE OF CONTENTS.

(a) SHORT TITLE—This Act may be cited as the '**Biological, Chemical, and Radiological Weapons Countermeasures Research Act**'.

(b) IN HONOR—This Act is enacted in honor of Robert Stevens, Thomas Morris Jr., Joseph Curseen, Kathy Nguyen, Ottilie Lundgren, and Lisa J. Raines, victims of terrorist attacks in the United States in 2001.

(c) TABLE OF CONTENTS—The table of contents of this Act is as follows:

'Sec. 1821. Federal tax incentives.
'Sec. 1822. Terror Weapon Countermeasure Purchase Fund.
'Sec. 1823. Patent term protection and exclusive marketing.
'Sec. 1824. Liability and indemnification.
'

'Subtitle C—Administrative Provisions
'Sec. 1841. Annual report.
'Sec. 1842. International conference on research to develop countermeasures.
Sec. 4. Tax incentives.
Sec. 5. Patent term protection and exclusive marketing.
Sec. 6. Approvals of certain drugs based on animal trials.
Sec. 7. Limited antitrust exemption.
Sec. 8. Incentives for the construction of biologics manufacturing facilities available for the production of countermeasures.
Sec. 9. Human clinical trials and drugs for rare diseases and conditions.
Sec. 10. Liability.

SEC. 2. FINDINGS.

Congress makes the following findings:

(1) The United States must be prepared with diagnostic and medical countermeasures in the event of the use of biological, chemical, and radiological weapons by terrorists and others against military and intelligence personnel, government officials, or civilians.

(2) The threat of biological and chemical weapons is real.

   (A) Members of the cult Aum Shinrikyo were responsible for chemical weapons attacks in Japan that killed 12 people and injured over 5,000 on March 20, 1995. In this attack, terrorists placed plastic bags of diluted sarin, a lethal nerve agent, on crowded subway trains during the morning rush-hour. It was found that sect members had legally stockpiled sodium cyanide and hundreds of tons of chemicals used to make sarin, including sodium fluoride, phosphorous trichloride, isopropyl alcohol, and acetonitrile. Aum Shinrikyo concealed its sarin manufacturing plant in a shrine to a sect goddess. Investigators also found a biological weapons research lab on the cult's compound. The facility contained an incubator, an electron microscope, a growth medium for fermenting or growing cultures, and cultures of the deadly botulinum toxin. Aum Shinrikyo members were apparently planning a more devastating offensive. The cult also released anthrax spores and botulinum in Tokyo nine times before it carried out its nerve gas attack. Aum's attempted germ attacks failed because the group's biologists cultured the strain of anthrax used to make vaccine, which is harmless. Had they used a potent culture, the outcome might have been very different. No one knows why the botulism attack failed. The horror is only magnified by the thought that individuals and nations would consider attacking others with such viruses. In October 1993, Shoko Asahara, head of the Aum Shinrikyo cult, and 40 followers traveled to Zaire, ostensibly to help treat Ebola victims.

But the group's real intention, according to an October 31, 1995, report by the Permanent Subcommittee on Investigations of the Senate, was probably to obtain virus samples, culture them and use them in biological attacks.

(B) Before the 2001 anthrax attacks, the most recent successful biological attack in the United States, which was not recognized as such at the time, was with salmonella. Followers of Bhagwan Shree Rajneesh put the bacteria in salad bars in restaurants in Dalles, Oregon, in 1984, sickening 750 people.

(C) There is a long and sordid history of chemical and biological weapons, including use during the First and Second World Wars, an accidental release of anthrax spores in 1979 from a Soviet military microbiological facility, use of mustard gas, tabun, and hydrogen cyanide by Iraq in the Iran-Iraq War and against the Kurds, and development by Iraq of an offensive biological weapons capability including anthrax and botulinum toxin. Before, during, and after the Second World War, the Soviet Union produced many tens of thousands of tons of chemical weapons (both nerve and blister agents). During the later half of the Cold War, Soviet scientists developed a series of new and more lethal 'third generation' nerve agents. Certain of these new agents produced and tested in pilot and experimental quantities in thelate 1980s and early 1990s were up to 10 times more lethal than VX and soman. Additionally, because these are binary agents, i.e., they consist of two relatively non-toxic chemicals that are mixed together when the weapon is armed to produce the lethal chemical agent, they can be manufactured at commercial chemical plants that manufacture fertilizers and pesticides. A new unitary agent was also developed that could be produced from accessible raw materials that are used in civilian industry and which cannot therefore be regulated by international experts. Although less lethal per unit weight than traditional nerve agents, agricultural organophosphate insecticides are available in enormous quantities and can be used as nerve agents.

(D) The United States bioterror weapons program focused on anthrax, botulinum toxin, brucellosis, tularemia, psittacosis, plagua, Venezuelan equine encephalitis, Q fever, cholera, dengue, shigellosis dysentery, glanders, and Rocky Mountain spotted fever. The United States Army concocted a botulinum toxin that was so toxic that a pound, if expertly dispersed, could kill 1,000,000,000 people. Botulinum toxin is 15,000 times more toxic than VX and 10,000 times more toxic than Sarin. The Soviet bioterror program involved 47 laboratories and 65,000 people. It focused on 52 different pathogens, including smallpox, anthrax, plague, Ebola and Marburg hemorrhagic fevers, yellow fever, tularemia, brucellosis, Q fever, botulinum toxin, and Venezuelan equine encephalitis. It created 2,000 strains of anthrax with 7,000 employees working on nothing but anthrax. It produced 20 tons of smallpox virus each year, created antibiotic resistant bacterial strains with odd properties to confuse diagnosis, plague bacteria that secreted diphtheria toxin and resisted antibiotics. The Iraqi bioterror program focused on anthrax, botulinum toxin, cholera, plague, gas gangrene,

Salmonella, ricin, staphylococcal enterotoxin, camelpox, cancer-causing molds called aflatoxins, rotavirus, and hemorrhagic conjunctivitis.

(E)   A Central Intelligence Agency report concluded that 'clandestine production of chemical and biological weapons for multiple casualty attacks raises no greater technical obstacles than does the clandestine production of chemical narcotics or heroin'. One of the aspects which makes chemical and biological agents such an attractive weapon for a terrorist is the high shock value of these weapons.

(F)   The Office of Technology Assessment estimated that 100 kilograms of anthrax released upwind in an American city could cause between 130,000 and 3,000,000 deaths, depending on the weather and other variables. This degree of carnage is in the same range as that forecast for a hydrogen bomb.

(3) The threat of terrorism using radiological weapons is real.

(A)   In April 2000, customs officers from Uzbekistan discovered 10 lead-lined containers at a remote border crossing with Kazakhstan. These containers were filled with enough radioactive material to make dozens of crude weapons, each capable of contaminating a large area for many years. The consignment was addressed to a company in Quetta, Pakistan, called Ahmadjan Haji Mohammed. Quetta, where border controls are virtually non-existent, is the main Pakistani crossing into southern Afghanistan and only a 6 hour drive from Kandahar.

(B)   In 1994 Czech police seized 3 kilograms of highly enriched uranium. During the same year German police seized 360 grams of plutonium. In 2001 Turkish police seized two men with 1.16 kilograms of weapons grade uranium. Russian general Alexander Ledbed claimed that 40 suitcase nuclear weapons were unaccounted for.

(C)   In 1995 Islamic Chechen rebels announced, and Russians confirmed, that they had planted a 30 pound shielded container holding the Cesium-137 core of a cancer treatment device in a Moscow park.

(D)   The International Atomic Energy Agency, a Vienna-based division of the United Nations, has documented almost 400 cases of trafficking in nuclear or radiological materials since 1993. Many such supplies are subject to few controls or are poorly guarded, particularly in the former Soviet Union. Reports also have cited weak protection of spent fuel at nuclear facilities in the United States. Other experts worry about the security of the nuclear facilities in Pakistan, India, and other developing countries. An estimated 1300 kilograms of highly enriched uranium and 180,000 kilograms of plutonium, the main fuels for a nuclear device, exists in civilian nuclear facilities around the world. There are nearly 450 nuclear power plants, nearly 300 nuclear research reactors, and 250 nuclear fuel cycle plants around the world.

(E)   In September 1987, scavengers broke into an abandoned cancer clinic in Goiania, Brazil and stole a medical device containing large amounts of radioactive cesium-137. An estimated 250 people were exposed to the source, eight developed radiation sickness, and four died.

(F) A crude but deadly radiation dispersal device (RDD) fashioned from stolen nuclear material (from a nuclear waster processor, a nuclear power plant, a university research facility, a medical radiotherapy clinic, or an industrial complex) and a few sticks of dynamite could spread radioactive material across an area without a nuclear detonation. Such a weapon could kill many, contaminate a square mile for10 years or more, and cause widespread panic. The Chernobyl nuclear reactor meltdown in 1986 resulted in the uninhabitability of a 6 mile belt around the reactor. That area is still uninhabitable today. It released about 400 times as much radioactivity at the Hiroshima bomb. Half of the atoms in a sample of cobalt-60 will disintegrate over a 5 year period, but it takes 430 years for half of the atoms in a sample of Americium-241 to decay.

(G) Even more threatening, during the Cold War the United States and the Soviet Union fashioned a few hundred portable nuclear weapons and some of the Soviet weapons might fall into the hands of terrorists.

(H) The panic at dispersal or detonation of such a device might well be much more damaging than the morbidity and mortality. Radiation is invisible and there is widespread fear of it. Few would understand the difference between a dirty and a nuclear bomb.

(I) Such a device or bomb can cause exposure to a variety of radioactive materials, including Plutonium, enriched or depleted Uranium, Radium, Cesium, Strontium, Cobalt, Iodine, Americium, etc.

(J) Such exposure can cause immediate death, as well as adverse effects on radiosensitive tissues, including suppression of white and red blood stem and platelet cells production. Acute Radiation Syndrome (ARS), Central Nervous System syndrome (CNS), gastrointestinal syndrome, and bone marrow radiation syndrome are early effects of substantial acute exposure to ionizing radiation. Leukemia and other forms of cancer can arise many years after exposure even to lower doses. Other symptoms include nausea, vomiting, hair loss, diarrhea, hemorrhages, and internal bleeding. The United States has only one hospital emergency room dedicated to treating patients exposed to radiation hazards, at Oak Ridge, Tennessee.

(K) Medical responses currently available with respect to exposure to radioactive materials are rather limited and can include use of chelation agents to speed secretion of radioactive metals from the body if radioactive material was swallowed or inhaled, preventive blocking of thyroid uptake of radioactive iodine by use of potassium iodine tablets, and use of Investigational New Drugs like Prussian Blue.

(L) The United States needs to develop additional medical responses, including antiemetics, hematological colony-stimulating factors, and chelating agents. The United States also needs to develop better means of assessing radiation exposure using new molecular, biological, physical and other technologies.

(M) The ill-defined and uncontrolled nature of radiation exposure and nuclear accidents usually causes a non-uniform exposure with the variable dose distribution complicating dosimetry, which is important for medical management of exposed patient with a need to determine the degree to which bone marrow or gastrointestinal stem cells have survived.

(4) The United States must take steps to prevent access to the biological and chemical agents and toxins and radiological materials by terrorists and others, but attacks may nonetheless occur. The United States needs to respond to attacks with well-coordinated public health measures. We also need a broad array of effective diagnostics and medicines to rapidly identify and treat those who are exposed to, or infected by, the agents, toxins, or materials.

(5) The United States faces a public health crisis with the spread of antibiotic resistant bacteria. This alone should lead us to take urgent action to develop new vaccines and medicines. The antibiotic vancomycin, our last line of defense against the often deadly bacterium, Staphylococcus aureus, is losing its effectiveness. Worldwide, many strains of S. aureus are already resistant to all antibiotics except vancomycin. Emergence of strains lacking sensitivity to vancomycin signifies that variants untreatable by every known antibiotic are on their way. S. aureus, a major cause of hospital-acquired infections, has thus moved one step closer to becoming an unstoppable killer. What is more, strains of at least three bacterial species capable of causing life-threatening illnesses (Enterococcus faecalis, Mycobacleriumn tuberculosis and Pseudomonas aeruginosa) already evade every antibiotic in the clinician's armamentarium, a stockpile of more than 100 drugs. In part because of the rise in resistance to antibiotics, the death rates for some communicable diseases (such as tuberculosis) have started to rise again, after having declined in the industrial nations.

(6) The possibility exists that terrorists or others will use biotechnology techniques to enhance the lethality of a biological agent. According to the Defense Science Board, 'Motivated researchers using advanced genetics techniques can engineer pathogens with unnatural characteristics that enhance their offensive properties by altering such characteristics as stability, dissemination properties, host range, contagiousness, resistance to drugs and vaccines, and persistence in the environment, among others'.

(7) Vaccines exist for some of the biological agents that might be used by terrorists and others, but these vaccines need substantial additional development. The development of new vaccines is a difficult, costly, and time-consuming endeavor with no assurance of success. In the last 25 years, the Federal Government though its efforts to protect the public health and the military against disease has successfully developed very few new vaccines. The development of vaccines against highly lethal bioterror agents may face far greater difficulties. For such vaccines often there may be no animal model or the animal will be of questionable value. The development of vaccines against many such disease agents will require clinical trials in countries where the disease agent in endemic and the prevalence of infection is sufficiently high to prove efficacy. The current United States vaccine against anthrax was formulated in the 1960s and licensed in 1970. Before and subsequent

to the licensing of this vaccine in the United States, additional preclinical and clinical studies have been conducted to confirm its safety and efficacy. The current Food and Drug Administration-licensed immunization schedule for the anthrax vaccine involves 6 doses over 18 months followed by yearly boosters. Since this is a cumbersome schedule for immunizing both military personnel and civilian laboratory workers and first responders at occupational risk of exposure to the biothreat from an anthrax attack, the Centers for Disease Control and Prevention has initiated multi-center studies to develop the next generation of the anthrax vaccine by reducing the number of doses and changing its route of administration. Additional early development phase studies of experimental recombinant and live attenuated anthrax vaccines are underway to determine their suitability, safety and efficacy.

(8) Treatments for those who are not protected by vaccines are often not effective. Inhalation anthrax (woolsorters' disease) results from inhaling anthrax spores disseminated from either a natural source or a biological attack and, if untreated, it is considered to be 99 percent fatal. Antibiotics and standard interventions provided after symptoms have developed rarely prevent a fatal outcome.

(9) The United States does not currently have available the diagnostics, drugs, and vaccines needed in the event of a bioterror attack. It has been estimated by the Defense Science Board that the United States is adequately protected with respect to only 13 of the top 50 pathogens that might be weaponized. For example, while the United States has a vaccine for smallpox, that vaccine has side effects and is one that cannot be well tolerated by many, and for those who are infected, the United States has no effective treatment. The United States has a treatment for early stage inhalation anthrax, but those treatments are ineffective when there are delays in diagnosis. The United States has very few products that are effective against viruses. The United States is not well protected with broad-spectrum antibiotics that are needed to deal with pathogens that have been modified or selected for antibiotic resistance. It takes more than 24 hours to diagnose many of the most dangerous pathogens.

The Government Performance and Results Act of 1993 specifically requires clear and quantifiable performance measures to gauge progress in monitoring and controlling its foreign visits and assignments program

DOE/IG-465
Inspection Report
Inspection of the Department of Energy's Export License Process for Foreign National Visits and Assignments
March 2000
U.S. Department of Energy, Office of the Inspector General, Office of Inspections

http://www.ig.doe.gov/pdf/ig0465.pdf

This report found that there was a lack of information in the Department's formal data gathering process. As a result, DOE officials were not aware of the precise number of foreign nationals visiting the Department's laboratories.

Department of Energy
DOE Needs to Improve Controls Over Foreign Visitors to Weapons Laboratories
September 1997
GAO/RCED-97-229

http://www.gao.gov/archive/1997/rc97229.pdf

"DOE Needs to Improve Controls Over Foreign Visitors to Weapons Laboratories" (GAO/RCED-97-229, September 1997). Essentially the laboratories had demonstrated the vulnerability of sensitive information being compromised.

I'll almost bet that somebody came out with a policy directive right after these reports were issued too.

We are handing these visas out like Halloween candy. I hear many of our Senators and Congressmen in strong support of foreign work visas, why? They claim that we need foreign labor to help the economy grow. Do you think that's the reason?

A smart guy could probably go online and with some hard work and tenacity, find out how many of the corporations that seek foreign labor also contribute to many campaigns. I'll bet it would be an amazing coincidence that many of these corporations also have donated to certain politicians. You could probably find that many of these corporations also received H-1B training grants. Of course, this is all coincidence. Corporations often give to both parties, and of course, it would only be a coincidence that they receive H-1B training grants.

Department of Homeland Security
Office of the Inspector General
Semiannual Report to the Congress
April 1, 2003–September 30, 2003

http://www.dhs.gov/interweb/assetlibrary/OIG_Fall_2003_SAR.pdf

All right, not every bit of news is bad. Take for example April 1, 2003 when several e-mails were sent out resulting in the release of a detainee. The Department of Homeland Security OIG conducted an investigation and concluded that an employee who had duties in both Citizenship and Immigration Services/Customs Enforcement sent an e-mail stating that a detainee's U.S. Citizenship had been established, thereby permitting the detainee's release.

The detainee had a prior conviction for kidnapping and surrendered himself two days later without incident.

A second e-mail was sent out to let them know it was an April fools joke, but the Duty Officer failed to see the April fools reference in the first e-mail and failed to read the second e-mail advising that the first e-mail was intended to be a joke.

The Duty Officer signed the internal paperwork that resulted in the detainee's unauthorized release from a local county jail. The employee was placed on paid leave from April 4 through October 27, 2003 and later an unpaid leave from October 20, 2003 through November 19, 2003.

Seven months paid leave and ~ four weeks unpaid leave for this incident. Now for the good news, at least this wasn't a terrorist that was released, because I don't think that they would have returned, do you?

The incident had been referred to the United States Attorney's Office for prosecution, but the matter was declined.

Now, what if somebody tried to warn us a year ago, two years ago, or even longer, how important the need to guard against the abuse of the visa system. Do you think we would have listened? Here's something from the 103d CONGRESS that we should have probably really paid a lot of attention to. I only wish we had a Congressional Medal for Intelligence because one should have been handed out here. By the way, this was from 1993, and it is so important that I included the entire Concurrent Resolution. If we only listened and did a better job!

http://frwebgate.access.gpo.gov/cgi-bin/getdoc.cgi?dbname=103_cong_bills&docid=f:hc119ih.txt

When searching—http://thomas.loc.gov enter the Word/Phrase—"H. CON. RES. 119"

103d CONGRESS
1st Session
H. CON. RES. 119

To urge the Secretary of State to provide to the Congress an emergency plan to vastly improve the visa issuance process of the Department of State to prevent terrorists from entering the United States.

IN THE HOUSE OF REPRESENTATIVES
July 13, 1993

Mr. Gilman submitted the following concurrent resolution; which was referred to the Committee on the Judiciary

CONCURRENT RESOLUTION

To urge the Secretary of State to provide to the Congress an emergency plan to vastly improve the visa issuance process of the Department of State to prevent terrorists from entering the United States.

Whereas recent terrorist acts in the United States have made it abundantly clear that terrorism has come to American soil, and now threatens the very security of the Nation;

Whereas it is evident from recent revelations that the State Department's current visa operations and procedures are not adequate to provide a modern front line defense to prevent terrorists from entering the United States under visas provided by United States embassies and consular posts around the world;

Whereas many overseas State Department posts are still using outdated and inefficient microfiche systems to maintain visa lookout and watch lists for known or suspected terrorists who may seek United States visas to travel to the United States;

Whereas the lookout list microfiche system is outdated, not easily maintained or updated in a timely fashion, is labor intensive and easily subject to human error, and is totally inadequate and outmoded in this era of modern communications and travel;

Whereas many United States embassy and consular posts are still on the outdated microfiche system in many areas of the world where the threat is great from terrorists and drug dealers or narcotics traffickers who may desire visas to enter the United States;

Whereas the microfiche visa lookout system has already resulted in the unfortunate and mistaken entry of radical Sheik Omar Abdel Rahman into the United States on a United States visa, despite his links to known terrorist activities prior to issuance of the visa;

Whereas the mistaken issuance of the visa to Sheik Rahman in error in Khartoum in 1990, despite the fact he was on the State Department's lookout list on microfiche at this post for possible terrorist links, has created numerous and serious problems for the United States, including his possible inspiration and encouragement of terrorism following his entry into the United States, both here and in Egypt by his followers;

Whereas several of Sheik Rahman's followers have been arrested in connection with the New York Trade Tower bombing or relating to a terrorist plot to attack the United Nations complex, New York City commuter tunnels, the Secretary General of the United Nations, and political leaders in the United States, and many of those arrested entered the United States with visas issued by the State Department;

Whereas the entry of Sheik Rahman into the United States by the mistaken issuance of a visa by the State Department has even reportedly strained our relations with the Government of Egypt;

Whereas it is also evident that the necessary information sharing within the State Department, and with other United States law enforcement and intelligence agencies on possible terrorists or other criminal elements, is not being conducted on an appropriate basis to make the visa lookout system current and effective enough to prevent possible terrorists from entering the United States with visas;

Whereas the shortcomings and failures in the current visa processing system at the Department of State have been well known by the Department for many years and no major overhaul, improvements, or recommendations to overhaul the system are forthcoming from the Department of State, the Inspector General, or the General Accounting Office for several months;

Whereas a 1991 Department of State Inspector General audit of the visa referral system at the Department found serious shortcomings in the automated visa lookout system (AVOLS), including "Information regarding foreign nationals with serious grounds for visa ineligibility" was not always in the automated visa lookout system even though government agencies had this information available;

Whereas the same 1991 audit also found that "At one post visited it was determined that not all convicted drug traffickers in the Drug Enforcement Agency local data base were in AVOLS";

Whereas the same 1991 audit went on to find that "The absence of this information (law enforcement data) poses a serious problem to the nonimmigrant visa process since it can result in the issuance of visas to dangerous and undesirable individuals.";

Whereas the Department of State, on the basis of the 1991 audit, has been on notice of the shortcomings in the visa lookout system for more than 2 years, and apparently little or no progress has been made to improve the system;

Whereas recently the Secretary of State has personally acknowledged the need to modernize the visa system to meet the new threat of terrorism directly targeted at the United States;

Whereas the American people demand and expect the Department of State to maintain an effective and modern system to prevent terrorists from obtaining visas to travel to the United States and threaten property, institutions, and lives in the United States; and

Whereas the current visa processing system and procedures at the Department of State are totally incapable in meeting the new threat of international terrorism to the United States and threaten the very security and safety of the United States: Now, therefore, be it

Resolved by the House of Representatives (the Senate concurring), That it is the sense of the Congress that the Secretary of State, within 60 days after the date of adoption of this resolution, should submit a report to the Congress setting forth an emergency plan to improve visa issuance procedures and equipment and to modernize the visa processing system including—

(1) short-term and immediate plans to modernize high threat United States posts around the globe now currently on outdated microfiche;

(2) plans to improve information sharing within the Department of State itself to keep the visa lookout system current and updated on possible terrorist who might seek visas to travel to the United States;

(3) plans to improve information sharing with other United States agencies to provide timely and efficient exchange of information for inclusion in the visa lookout system to prevent terrorists and other alien criminal elements from gaining access to the United States under visas issued by United States embassies and consular posts overseas;

(4) a date certain when the Department of State will resume checking the criminal record histories of visa applicants with the Federal Bureau of Investigation, prior to issuance of any visa, as was the case prior to 1991; and

(5) long-term plans to make the visa lookout and watch system a modern and effective tool to prevent terrorists, and other criminal elements, from gaining easy access to the United States under visas issued by United States embassies or overseas consular posts.

<all>

I think that the amazing part of this was that it came out July 13, 1993. Unfortunately, nobody listens.

Chapter 7

Nobody Seems to Really Care

GAO
Testimony before the Senate Judiciary Subcommittee on Immigration, Border Security and Citizenship
Border Security
New Policies and Increased Interagency Coordination Needed to Improve the Visa Process, Statement of Jess T. Ford, Director, International Affairs and Trade
GAO-03-1013T
For Release on Delivery Expected at 2:30 p.m. EDT Tuesday, July 15, 2003

http://www.gao.gov/new.items/d031013t.pdf

Don't get mad at me here, I want to bounce back in time a little and go over a GAO report from 2003. The July 15, 2003 report on "Border Security—New Policies and Increased Interagency Coordination Needed to Improve Visa Process" is where I would like to really focus.

The reason I want to focus on this report, is because a lot of people (lobbyists, corporations) are beginning to wine about the reduced number of visas and how quotas should be up because of the need for foreign workers. Remember, these guys make their money off immigration, so when you reduce it, they get a pain in their wallet.

This report keeps coming back to me like the first song you hear on the radio in the morning, you can't get rid of it. I think it bothers me so much because I worry that lobbying, campaign contributions and good old fashion greed are still keeping us at great risk. Remember, this is a July 2003 report, it's not like its 20 years old and we are still facing some critical issues on immigration.

The report noted that the process broke down because information is not shared between the State Department, immigration and law enforcement agencies. The information they are speaking about concerns the revocation of visas.

The report talks about 240 visas that were revoked because of terrorism concerns and that there were numerous cases where the revocations did not reach the appropriate units within INS and the FBI.

Now I know that doesn't seem like a lot of people we are talking about, but if you are going to issue any visa you should make sure there is no threat. In this case, there were some pretty interesting findings, (synopsis)

- Appropriate units of the INS and FBI did not always receive timely notification of the revocations
- Lookouts were not consistently posted to the watch lists
- 30 individuals whose visas were revoked on terrorism grounds entered the United States and may still remain in the country
- INS investigators were not usually notified of individuals with revoked visas who had entered the United States and therefore did not open investigations on them
- The FBI did not investigate individuals with revoked visas unless these individuals were also in the TIPOFF
- There wasn't notification between the State Department and the INS or it was not in a timely manner in 43 of the 240 cases. In 47 other cases, the notice came via cable, which took an average of 12 days.
- When the INS was notified, they took about a day to post the information in their database. When they weren't notified, the inspectors at ports of entry could not know these visas had been revoked. The State Department neglected to enter the revocation action for 64 of the 240 cases into its own watch list.
- GAO's analysis of INS arrival and departure data indicates 29 individuals entered the U.S. before their visas could be revoked and may still remain in the country, however the FBI says none of these 30 individuals posed a threat since they were not in the TIPOFF (State operated interagency terrorist watch list that FBI's Foreign Terrorist Tracking Task Force monitors). INS inspectors prevented 14 others from entering because they were on a watch list because of revocation or other lockout.
- INS didn't open the cases because they weren't notified State revoked the visas because of terrorism concerns. In 10 cases, INS said it would be challenging to remove them. Homeland Security officials said it is unresolved legally about the revocation of a visa after entering on that visa—out-of-status.
- FBI wasn't concerned about the revoked visas unless they were in TIPOFF; they have their own system to monitor.

I'm really upset with the loss of jobs, but it actually frightens you when you think about how many holes there are in the system.

We have corporations and lobbyists and all sorts of special interest groups calling for people to come here and work. We're putting profit before safety and not a real lot of people seem to have timely information or a rapid warning system or share the information immediately.

The report also states "These weakness diminish the effectiveness of the visa process in keeping potential terrorists out of the United States". This statement stands by itself.

U.S. Department of State
Press Statement
Adam Ereli, Deputy Spokesman
Washington, DC
April 2, 2004
http://www.state.gov/r/pa/prs/ps/2004/31103.htm

The State Department and Department of Homeland Security want to extend for two years the requirement for Visa Waiver Program (VWP) countries, biometrics issued on or after October 26, 2004. These countries can't produce biometric passports due to—you're going to like this—"technical difficulties".

The solution may be to virtually halt the entire process until they fix the technical difficulties. Want to see how fast they get the system up and running. The Department of State and Department of Homeland Security want a two-year extension for these countries.

The Enhanced Border Security and Visa Entry Reform Act of 2002 set a deadline of October 26, 2004 for this system to be in place. The new and improved current plan is to get it running by the end of 2005. Do I hear 2006, 2006 going once…

While were on the subject of visas, let's look at the system. The article is about a visa lottery—"Diversity Visa Lottery 2004 (DV-2004) Results".

Diversity Visa Lottery 2004 (DV-2004) Results
http://unitedstatesvisas.gov/visanews/index.html

The Kentucky Consular Center in Williamsburg, Kentucky registered and notified the winners of the DV-2004 Diversity Visa Lottery. It's a fun game and it works like this, section 203 (c) of the Immigration and Nationality Act makes 50,000 permanent residents visas available.

The lottery runs for one month, and has millions of players. Some people can't qualify if they were received outside the mail-in period or disqualified.

This is exactly what this is, a free ticket for citizenship.

Chapter 8
Flavor of the Month

What if somebody told you that the odds were way against you to be re-trained and find a job in a new field before your unemployment ran out?

I always hear the DOL praising their one stop career centers. Let's take a look at how good the one-stops really are.

We have a real problem with the way we are trying to re-train our workforce. When somebody loses a job, they need to be re-trained very quickly with the skills necessary to survive in the workforce.

First, they can't goof around filling out forms, waiting for approval for re-training, or being turned away. Workers, have twenty-six weeks of unemployment benefits before they are hosed.

People used to have one year to find gainful employment when they were laid-off before running out of benefits. That stopped a long time ago, because we thought a year was too long and that people were milking the system. So, we reduced the time down to six months and expected the worker would move their tail to find another job.

We didn't count on permanent job loss, outsourcing, off-shoring or any of the other fun ingredients in job hunting when they reduced the benefit time to six months. Many people in this recession were out for a year and even two years before finding work. I guess it was because—THERE WERE NO JOBS TO FIND!

With the system set up as it is, the unemployed have six months to find a job or their lives start to become dismantled. I won't even get into the horror stories about unemployment, because I'm sure everybody knows somebody who has been hurt during this recession. I used the word hurt, because the current system is like going through an accident.

I can hear a lot of people now saying how dare you? We are proud of our system and it is much better than it was. We have made great strides, improvements, etc....I guess my response to that would be "let's outsource your job, and we'll come back in a year or so for your opinion".

Why do you think they call them One-Stop Centers, it's because you'll probably you'll never want to stop there twice?

Anyway, the system is pretty cool. It goes something like this (may vary), you get laid-off and go to a One-Stop center, receive an orientation, send in a letter to explain why you need re-training, hunt for a school that you can go to, get approval (if money is available for re-training—else pray), go to school, get job immediately, and continue with life.

Here come the problems. Many people have to send in a letter to explain why they need re-training. Let's waste a few weeks, while you justify why you won't be able to find a job.

Then, find a school. Many trade school prices vary. If you have x amount of dollars allotted for your training, you better find an affordable school. If you don't, you'll be paying the difference if you want to be re-trained.

Then you get approval, if the money is there. During this recession, or economic recovery that is over for years long, many states run out of dollars for training. If you wanted to go to school, you can forget, unless you pay.

By the time you get approved, it isn't unheard of that two months went by. That leaves you with four months. Four months to learn a skill (if your lucky) that will enable you to support yourself and your family.

That just about does it for time. Find a job, go away and now you're not counted on the books as unemployed. Offer may vary but in a nutshell it's close.

Do you really think that in a few months of re-training you are going to find that dream job like the one you lost? Do you think that you'll be trained well enough so that you can earn the same money or earn a better living than you were? You're lucky if you can find a job.

I stopped at the One-Stop center in my state to inquire about what training programs they offered. I was told that the only training available at the time was through state schools. They had a program that was based on your ability to pay for training. You can go to any state school and sign up for a class (if there's room).

What if the class I wanted wasn't offered until the next semester? What if the class wasn't offered at all? What if it will take more than one class for me to re-train? What if the classes were offered but one at one school and one at another? It didn't seem as promising as it sounded.

The other problem was time. Colleges aren't based on drive through training. You have around four months, maybe five to re-train if you can get all the courses you need. There aren't a lot of colleges around that provide ready mix training within four months.

All of the new and improved job training programs are trying to link to colleges. That's a great idea if you are unemployed for two to four years, but all you are really doing is giving the money to the state colleges and saying "Happy Birthday".

Well, I guess that leaves private schools to re-train. Many private schools depend on the states to send them students; in fact, a big chunk of their business is from state funding. Without the state sending them students, they would have a hard time keeping the doors open.

I can remember years ago, schools offered placement. Not placement assistance but placement. Now, many of these schools only offer placement assistance. No guarantees. Remember, it's education but it's a business first.

So by the time you done with your training, times up. You better have a job waiting for you because you're probably pretty close to being out of money. Unless of course Washington has a solution to solve the economic disaster, it called an extension. Keep your fingers crossed.

There are a lot of schools out there that are pretty good. They do a good job with the training and placement but there are a lot of bad ones too. There are schools out there that offer training programs that are so fast paced, that you would probably have a hard time trying to absorb everything that's thrown at you. Since it's only going to be your career, it's not like it matters.

I think the worse part of this is that the odds are against you that you are going finish a training program and find employment in that field. During this recession, the DOL was sending thousands of students through computer training programs.

There were some real problems with sending people who were laid off through computer school. First, there were really no jobs in the computer field however; the schools just kept cranking out students. From the beginning of this downturn, the placement kept getting worse and worse.

The DET pretty much shut off Web design, because you couldn't buy a job in that part of the computer field. The placement rates were so bad; they completely cut off Web design training.

The other problem was that there were hundreds of thousands of experienced computer professionals that were laid off and they were aggressively looking for employment. What chance do you think you had if you were just trained going up against a guy with 15 to 20 years experience who was desperate enough to take an entry-level job?

You don't think that the companies enjoyed this? Here was a workforce desperate for jobs, and companies could pick and choose from the best of the best. They could put jobs in the paper that required you to have a MA of PHD in computer science and they were willing to pay about a third of what they normally would in a good economy.

The problem was, that the training agencies had to send people somewhere, so they kept sending them to computer schools. Even as many of the placement rates hit rock bottom, the states kept farming them out, because that was all they know how to do.

I've seen people go through computer training programs and end up at sub shops, lumber stores, or end up getting jobs at gas stations. Tax dollars went into training these people, like 8 to 12 thousand dollars per student, and the return on investment was a minimum wage job at a convenience store.

Did you really need to spend thousands of dollars to train someone to work at a home goods store? I watched many students finish training programs and the DET seemed to turn the other way because at least they were off unemployment.

Now the other part wrong with the training programs was the timeframe. It's like putting 5lbs. of manure in a 2 lb. Bag. Something is going to give. You had students on the fast track training programs, and I really mean fast track. Schools were training in 8 weeks sometimes even less for computer training. Imagine having to study 1 computer manual a week for eight weeks. Each manual was approximately 600 to 800 pages.

Part of the training was to provide 8 modules of training in 8 weeks. Now of course there were schools that provided the same training over a longer timeframe, and they also charged for it. Many schools offered training programs with shorter timeframes.

This wasn't any different from H-1B training, I went online at looked at H-1B training that wasn't measured in weeks but in hours. Just look at some of the grants that were given out under the program and calculate the hours.

Why would you keep sending people for computer training? People only have six months of unemployment; you can't send them to college. Most of the people laid off were from the computer field, so sending them to tractor-trailer training schools wasn't going to happen. Most of the schools out there trained in computers or medical office, and most men didn't want to become medical office administrators.

Here we went around in a circle, laid off from the computer field and back at school trying to re-train in the computer field. Not the greatest plan we could have devised.

If you think the DOL was doing a great job with this displaced workforce, the following reports will help re-enforce what you probably already knew. I did find some stuff in here that I even thought was pretty amusing and that I felt worth sharing.

Semiannual Report to the Congress
Volume 50
Office of the Inspector General\
U.S. Department of Labor
April 1–September 30, 2003

http://www.oig.dol.gov/public/reports/sar/50-April%202003-September%202003.pdf

On page 8 of this 57-page report, there is a section "Services and Outcomes of the Dislocated Worker Program Generally Positive, but Improvements can be made".

In this section, the reports explains how 65percent of the participants sampled, the career One-Stop Centers were unable to demonstrate that participants were unlikely to return to their previous occupations, which is a core requirement for the eligibility in the program. This issue was previously an issue from a June 2000 report.

That's a pretty high number 65percent of people won't be going back to their old occupation. I also found it comforting that this issue was identified three years earlier and it's still an issue

The report also states "One out of every four sampled participants was still enrolled in the program by the end of the audit fieldwork. These participants had exhausted their unemployment compensation, spent at least 514 days in the program (with some participants exceeding 700 days in the program), and received minimal assistance after completing training".

On page 10, the report further details how people who participated in the Dislocated Worker Program were not as positive as they were about the Job Training Partnership Act Program, they were not positive about job-finding assistance, which is a primary function of WIA.

On page 9 of the report, the OIG found questionable practices at New Mexico One-Stop Career Center. It seems that at the New Mexico Department of Labor (NMDOL) Las Cruces One-Stop Career Center that there was a complaint of impropriety. Allegations of concerns of the operation/management of the center, participant eligibility, state vehicles being used for nonofficial business, nepotism, and the requiring of employees to participate in religious meetings and read religious books.

OIG found evidence to support failure to follow policies and procedures for processing entitlement applications for family members of the NMDOL employees, misuse of center vehicles, and religious activities by center officials during business hours. The NMDOL generally agreed with the findings, and has taken appropriate corrective actions. However, they did not address the issue of Career Center employees keeping state vehicles at their residences.

If that information wasn't enough to bother you, the next section did on page 15–16 of the report will. This section dealt with the "Lack of Statutory Authority Limits DOL's Role in Verifying Foreign Labor Certification". The Employment and Training Administration is responsible for approving applications by employers that may allow immigrants to work in the U.S. The review of the H-1B in 1996 and the H-2B program in 1998 still show concerns about the following;

- Permanent Labor Certification—an electronic filing system could lead to fraud due to fewer controls over the application information
- H-1B Specialty Workers—employers have to declare that they will pay foreign workers appropriate wages. ETA's must approve the application without the

authority to validate information on the application. ETA's role adds little value to the process of protecting American jobs and wages.

- H-2A seasonal and temporary agricultural workers—The H-2A certification process is ineffective in ensuring U.S. workers jobs are protected.

"This report, as well as our prior reports, continues to demonstrate the Department's limited role in the labor certification process adds little value to the process of protecting American jobs and wages. (OA Report No. 06-03-007-03-321, issued September 30, 2003)".

Some of these issues have been around for close to a decade. Stuff like this is why people bounce off the wall. Can you imagine if a recommendation was made to you and almost ten years later you still didn't get around to it.

Let me stop for a minute and we can reflect on some numbers. The President wants allow ~10 million or so illegal immigrants the opportunity to enter work programs in the U.S. The President doesn't support an amnesty policy like many of Washington's finest, absolutely not an amnesty.

I was kind of wondering a couple of things about the word "illegal" in the term illegal immigrant. I always thought that had a meaning like—"jumped the border". I was under the impression that illegal was not legal. That if you were here illegally, you were already a CRIMINAL.

Now according to the policy, illegal immigrants who are here illegally, meaning not legally, meaning criminal, would be allowed to continue to work in the U.S. I think in Washington, it's called something like the guest worker program.

I have heard estimates of between 12–15 million Americans are looking for jobs. Jobs are permanently being lost everyday to new and improved created schemes, and we're going to give a green light to ILLEGAL immigrants.

I'm back on this tangent about this new immigration policy, because what would you possibly want to do this for? We have just gone through some of the worst few years imaginable and this is how you solve the job problem with an immigration policy like this?

Chapter 9
All Talk

I hear so many public officials talking about the improvements made in the federal government over the last few years. I listen to them talk about the great strides we have been making to ensure that the economy, safety of the nation and the overall well being of the American people.

The truth is that almost nothing improves, in many cases matters get worse.

Semiannual Report to the Congress
October 1, 2003–March 31, 2004
Volume 51
Office of the Inspector General
U.S. Department of Labor

http://www.oig.dol.gov/public/reports/sar/51-October%202003-March%202004%201.pdf

OIG Semiannual Report to Congress—October 1, 2003–March 31, 2004 Volume 51. Vulnerabilities in DOL Foreign Labor Certification Programs, the OIG states a concern about the abuse of the DOL foreign labor certification programs and the associated risk with foreign nationals who enter the United States by fraudulent means.

DOL is required to approve an application for the H-1B specialty worker program unless the application is "incomplete or obviously inaccurate".

Investigations, which have resulted in prison terms for immigration attorneys, immigration brokers, and defendants with organized crime ties charged with submitting false labor certifications, visa fraud, and alien smuggling.

Immigration is a profitable business. Billions of dollars are being made off immigrants entering the United States for work, everybody wants in on a piece of the action. The ink didn't dry on the paper when they lowered the number of H-1B's entering the United States before everybody started yelling to increase the numbers.

Here, you have an agency stating what I heave been speaking about, the concern of foreign nationals entering the United States. Do you think anyone will listen to the warnings? By the way, this isn't the first time that the OIG/DOL has expressed its concerns on foreign labor certification, and I'm sure it won't be the last.

The report also states that the OIG continues to uncover crimes of this type and also involve the creation of fictitious companies and documents using fraudulently obtained Social Security Numbers.

In addition, OIG evaluated H-2A workers nationwide in 2001 and found that many of these workers abandoned their jobs and were not reported to government authorities.

Greed. We are putting profit in front of the security of a nation. You can write this off, but let's take a look back to 9/11 and see if we have actually learned anything. Remember, the OIG report was up to March 31, 2004.

In 2004 the OIG is still expressing concern about foreign nationals entering the United States on visas. When are we going to learn?

U.S. Department of Energy
Office of the Inspector General
Office of Audit Services
Audit Report
Safeguards Over Sensitive Technology
DOE/IG-0635
January 2004

http://www.ig.doe.gov/pdf/ig-0635.pdf

The OIG reviewed 200 Cooperative Research and Development Agreements (CRADA) and Work-for-Others projects and determined that:

- In several agreements, two national laboratories Sandia and Los Alamos concluded that there was no foreign involvement. OIG through project documents concluded that foreign parties were involved. As a consequence, necessary safeguards may not have been implemented.
- At Sandia, required security classification reviews for six classified agreements were not submitted or were not approved by the Department in a timely manner.
- Although laboratory officials told OIG they routinely consult prohibited party lists, there was no indication in any project files reviewed that comparisons to lists had been made.
- Los Alamos and Oak Ridge assigned foreign nationals, three from sensitive countries to seven agreements involving subject matter on sensitive technology lists.
- Sandia had not conducted required counterintelligence reviews, Los Alamos relied on technology partnerships and classified personnel—not counterintelligence officials to identify CRADA related counterintelligence issues, Oak Ridge conducted

reviews as required. OIG was not able to reconcile the reasons for inconsistent application of Department policy.

These are our national laboratories that involve missions ranging from defense to research in physical sciences. You might think they would actually follow policy. This isn't the first time we have seen this though, the OIG report "Inspection of the Department of Energy's License Process for Foreign National Visits and Assignments (DOE/IG-0465, March 2000) identified a lack of clarity in the Departments guidance. December 2002, OIG reported two national laboratories had not adequately controlled unclassified visits and assignments by foreign nationals (DOE/IG-0579).

Not many improvements in four years.

Let's stick with the Department of Energy for a little while, because there are a few more issues that the 2004 audits found. Remember, these are our national laboratories, some of the nations most secret and sensitive work is conducted here.

U.S. Department of Energy
Office of the Inspector General
Office of Audit Services
Audit Report
The Department's Basic Protective Force Training Program
DOE/IG-0641
March 2004
http://www.ig.doe.gov/pdf/ig-0641.pdf

"The Department of Energy has 4,000 armed personnel responsible for securing the Department's nuclear materials, weapons, and national security-related information.

Results of Audit

- Each of the 10 sites eliminated or substantially modified 2 or more blocks of instruction. At one site, about 40 percent of the required 320 hours of basic security force training had been eliminated by deleting courses and modifying delivery methods
- Only one site conducted basic training on the use of a shotgun, despite the fact that a number of sites used the weapon for breaching and other purposes
- None of the sites included instruction in rappelling even though it was part of the special response training
- Seven of the sites modified prescribed training techniques by reducing the intensity or delivery method for skills that some security experts characterized as critical, such as handcuffing, hand-to-hand combat, and vehicle assaults."

I strongly recommend reading the entire report from the OIG/DHS, "An Evaluation of the Security Implications of the Visa Waiver Program" Office of Inspections, Evaluations, & Special Reviews OIG-04-26 April 2004—Department of Homeland Security.

I'm going to go right to the heart of this report because we are spending billions of dollars on security, databases, staff, and thousands of other associated costs fighting the war on terror. You can turn on a television or radio without hearing how we are increasing security somewhere to fight the war on terror.

Page 25 of this report—Stolen Passports are Returned to Travelers. Point of entry inspectors cited a problem, if an inspector identifies a lost or stolen passport while interviewing an applicant for entry—for example one that has been photo substituted or otherwise altered, the applicant will be denied entry, BUT the fraudulent document must be given back to the traveler. The traveler could return to the foreign port of departure with the document in hand.

This is so distressing that you almost can't believe we are this dumb. It's like giving them a second chance to try to get into the country again, maybe by an inexperienced inspector who won't catch the document.

The recommendation of the OIG to the Under Secretary for Border and Transportation Security was to issue a guidance policy to seize fraudulent passports. I can't even believe that the Office of the Inspector General has to recommend to the Under Secretary of Transportation and Border security that they should actually seize fraudulent passports.

Page 29 of the report deals with Point of Entry (POE) training. The report explains how inspectors attend a 12-week training program at the Federal Law Enforcement Training Center. In this program, inspectors only receive only one day of passport fraud training. New inspectors learn most of these skills on the job and new inspectors make mistakes that seasoned inspectors would avoid.

Compounding the training issue is the problem with attrition. At the bottom of the page, the attrition rates are listed as follows;

- FY 00: 46 out of 453 = 10.2 percent
- FY 01: 67 out of 453 = 14.8 percent
- FY 02: 96 out of 460 = 20.9 percent
- FY 03: 73 out of 471 = 15.5 percent

With the attrition rate of seasoned inspectors being so high, it even leaves more room for error. Add to this mistakes made by new inspectors and you have a system that is in desperate need of repair. It only takes one mistake to create a crisis.

Now to get on with the rest of this report, the Visa Waiver Program enables travelers of certain countries to enter the United States for tourism or business for 90 days without having to obtain a visa.

This program is a plagued with problems that must be addressed immediately. The following are some of the problems noted in this report, which are of high importance to the security of the nation;

- It is not clear within DHS or other agencies who is in charge of the Visa Waiver Program (VWP)
- Border and Transportation Security (BTS) is unable to comply with the mandate to conduct country review of each VWP designated country
- BTS' lack of readiness to conduct reviews directly undercuts its ability to assess the most serious security problem inherent in this program—lost and stolen passports (LASP).
- A potential security weakness in fraudulent use of VWP passports to bypass the United States Visitor and Immigrant Status Indicator Technology (US-VISIT) procedures

Virtually all those familiar with Visa Waiver Program operations told the OIG that lost and stolen passports is the greatest security problem associated with the VWP. Alien smuggling gangs routinely use fraudulent VWP passports to bring in illegal immigrants and their escorts into the United States.

No data has ever been collected on the misuse, because there has never been a requirement to do so.

OIG was told that criminals consider the VWP passport a very valuable commodity.

On March 11, 2004 a copy of this report was sent to BTS for review and a 30 day response was requested. As of April 20, 2004 BTS never replied with comments. An attempt was made to contact BTS but there were no replies. OIG considers all these matters unresolved.

Chapter 10

When All Else Fails, Pour Millions Into the System

What follows is a list of funds awarded to dislocated workers, as well as a few other associated awards. Note: This list does not include partnerships, competitive grant awards, etc.

http://www.doleta.gov/whatsnew/new_releases/

Period January 2003–April 2004

Labor Secretary Elaine L. Chao Announces $1.5 Million in Aid for Dislocated Maine Workers—April 15, 2004

Labor Department Gives Maine An Additional $2.6 Million in Trade Funds—March 31, 2004

U.S. Labor Secretary Elaine L. Chao Announces Grants of Over $1.3 Million for Oregon Workers—February 17, 2004

U.S. Labor Secretary Elaine L. Chao Announces $2.3 Million Grant To Aid Dislocated New Hampshire Workers—February 05, 2004

U.S. Labor Secretary Elaine L. Chao Announces Nearly $970,000 in Aid for Dislocated Oklahoma Workers—February 5, 2004

U.S. Labor Secretary Announces Grants of Nearly $2.7 Million for Dislocated Idaho Workers—January 15, 2004

Labor Secretary Elaine L. Chao Announces $1 Million Grant to Aid Dislocated Maine Workers—January 13, 2004

Labor Secretary Elaine L. Chao Announces Grant to Help Trade-Impacted Workers in West Virginia—Dec. 22, 2003

U.S. Labor Secretary Announces Grant of More Than $1.1 Million for Dislocated Mississippi Workers—December 15, 2003

Labor Secretary Announces $695,000 Grant To Aid Dislocated Workers in Connecticut—December 15, 2003

Labor Secretary Announces $8 Million Grant to Aid Alaska Workers Affected by Declining Fishing Industry—December 15, 2003

U.S. Secretary of Labor Announces $4.2 Million Grant To Aid Dislocated Georgia Workers—December 15, 2003

U.S. Labor Secretary Announces Grants of Nearly $1.3 Million for Dislocated Iowa Workers—December 15, 2003

Labor Secretary Announces $1.3 Million Grant to Aid Dislocated Connecticut Workers—November 26, 2003

Labor Secretary Elaine L. Chao Announces $512,796 To Aid Dislocated Vermont Workers—November 26, 2003

U.S. Labor Secretary Announces $15 Million In Grants For Dislocated High-Tech and Transportation Workers In California—November 26, 2003

Labor Secretary Elaine L. Chao Announces $7.4 Million Grant To Aid Dislocated Missouri Workers—November 20, 2003

Labor Secretary Elaine L. Chao Announces $1.5 Million Grant To Help Trade-Impacted Washington Workers Pay Health Insurance—November 19, 2003

Labor Secretary Elaine L. Chao Announces $12 MillionFor Disaster Aid In Wake Of California Wildfires—November 19, 2003

Labor Secretary Elaine L. Chao Announces $429,000 Grant To Aid Dislocated Arkansas Workers—November 18, 2003

Labor Secretary Elaine L. Chao Announces Nearly $1.2 Million To Aid Dislocated Wisconsin Farmers—November 4, 2003

Labor Secretary Elaine L. Chao Announces $340,206 Grant To Aid Dislocated Massachusetts Workers—November 4, 2003

Labor Secretary Elaine L. Chao Announces $998,000 Grant To Aid Dislocated Idaho Workers—October 27, 2003

U.S Labor Secretary Announces Additional Funds of $442,500 To Aid Dislocated Workers in Maine

Labor Secretary Elaine L. Chao Announces $6.8 Million National Emergency Grant for Texas Workers

<u>Labor Secretary Elaine L. Chao Announces $4.6 Million Grant To North Carolina To Continue Aid For Laid Off Burlington Workers</u>

<u>Labor Secretary Elaine L. Chao Announces $1.5 Million Grant To Aid Dislocated Montana Workers</u>

Labor Secretary Elaine L. Chao Announces $6.8 Million National Emergency Grant for Texas Workers

U.S. Labor Secretary Elaine L. Chao Announces $5 Million Grant For Dislocated Massachusetts Workers

Labor Secretary Elaine L. Chao Announces Grant To Aid Green Bay Area Workers

Labor Secretary Elaine L. Chao Announces $3.2 Million Grant To Aid Pillowtex Workers In Virginia

Labor Secretary Elaine L. Chao Announces $20.6 Million In Grants To Aid Pillowtex Workers In North Carolina

Labor Secretary Elaine L. Chao Announces $4.1 Million Grant To Aid South Central Wisconsin Workers

U.S. Labor Dept. Announces Assistance for Kimball Manufacturing Workers in Boise, Idaho

U.S. Labor Dept. Announces Assistance for Mackie Design, Inc., Workers in Woodinville, Wash.

U.S. Labor Dept. Announces Assistance for Premier Industries, Inc., Workers in Dallas, Ore.

U.S. Labor Dept. Announces Assistance for Intalco Aluminum Corp. Workers in Ferndale, Wash.

U.S. Labor Dept. Announces Assistance for Shinei USA, Inc., Workers in Hillsboro, Ore.

U.S. Labor Dept. Announces Assistance for Intalco Aluminum Corp. Workers in Ferndale, Wash.

Labor Grant Will Aid Dislocated South Dakota Workers

Labor Grant Will Aid Dislocated Washington Workers

Labor Grant Will Aid Dislocated Vermont Workers

Labor Grant Will Aid Dislocated Texas Workers

Labor Grant Will Aid Dislocated Rhode Island Workers

Labor Grant Will Aid Dislocated Oklahoma Workers

Labor Grant Will Aid Dislocated Utah Workers

Labor Grant Will Aid Dislocated Arkansas Workers

Labor Grant Will Aid Dislocated California Workers

Labor Grant Will Aid Dislocated Arizona Workers

Labor Grant Will Aid Dislocated Wisconsin Workers

Labor Grant Will Aid Dislocated Colorado Workers

Labor Grants Will Aid Dislocated Massachusetts Workers

Labor Grant Will Aid Dislocated South Carolina Workers

New Labor Grant To Minnesota Will Help Trade-Impacted Workers Pay For Health Insurance

New Labor Grant To Maryland Will Help Trade-Impacted Workers Pay For Health Insurance

It was kind of cool, here I was reading about all the money that was handed out to dislocated workers and this was for a little more than one year. If you go back further, it gets insane. This is only additional money on top of the regular expenditures allocated for workers.

Looking at these labor grants fall from the sky is so annoying, because at the end of each one of these is a person. Think of the people behind each of these and you see how our policies have taken a toll on the workers and their families.

On the website was a link to a speech made by the president. Let's take a look at the plan. Now keep in mind the recession has been going on for over four years. Sooner or later, even if you did nothing things have to improve. Here are some quotes from the speech.

Jobs and Economic Growth
President Discusses Economy and Job Training in North Carolina
April 5, 2004

http://www.whitehouse.gov/news/releases/2004/04/20040405-3.html

Page 4 paragraph 6

"We've had strong economic growth. This economy is growing. Inflation is low, interest rates are low. Manufacturing activity is on the increase. Homeownership rates are the highest ever. Isn't that a wonderful thought?".

Page 5 paragraph 2

"We have a strategy to make sure the economy stays strong. Let me share some of the ingredients of that strategy with you. First, in order for us to keep jobs at home, in order for us to make sure the job market expands, we've got to make sure the legal system is fair. Frivolous and junk lawsuits make it hard to expand the job base. The United States Congress must pass class-action lawsuit reform, asbestos reform, for the sake of creating new jobs. Tort reform is necessary."

Page 5 paragraph 5

"Good trade policy is necessary to keep jobs at home. There's a tendency to say, gosh, the jobs are going overseas, therefore let's isolate ourselves from the world. I think that's a mistake. Many small businesses rely upon being able to export. Farmers all across this country need to export their product. We're good at things, see. We're good at growing things. We're good at building things. And therefore, rather than isolate ourselves, we ought to take a different policy. We ought to make sure the playing field is level for our exporters."

Page 6 paragraph 1

"In order to make sure the economy is strong, we need spending discipline in Washington. I've laid out a plan to cut the deficit in half over five years. It's going to require the United States Congress not to overspend. And I look forward to working with them."

Page 6 paragraph 2

"Finally, another thing we need to do is we need an energy policy in this country. If you're a person trying to—if you're a manufacturer who relies upon energy, it's awfully hard to expand your job base if you're worried about whether or not the electricity system that you rely upon is modern. It's hard to expand your job base if you rely upon natural gas. It's hard to rely upon sound energy when we're dependent on foreign sources of energy. (Applause.) In order to make sure that the economy stays strong and people can find work here at home, the Congress needs to pass the energy plan we submitted, which will encourage more conservation, which will encourage our electricity system to become modernized, but—which will allow us to use clean coal technologies and to explore for natural gas so we're less dependent on foreign sources of energy. (Applause.)"

Page 6 paragraph 5

"For example, the average car today has 27 on-board computers. And in some cases, our cars have more raw computing power than that which was used to send the Apollo astronauts to the moon. Now, that's a pretty interesting thought, isn't it? Which means, if you're an automobile repair guy—(laughter)—you better know something about computers. (Laughter.) Or if you're an automobile manufacturer. In other words, this is the kind of sophisticated level that is necessary for our workers."

Page 9 paragraph 4

"The main worker training program is called the Workforce Investment Act. That's the primary—(applause.) Yes, there you go. (Laughter.) The program spends about $4 billion a year in grants on states—to states. Money from those grants go to about 3,500 state and local one-stop centers around the country. Perhaps some of you who have been looking for work or help have gone to a one-stop center. They're smart things to do. See, those one-stop centers have been providing employment services, advice, job search assistance, resume writing. In other words, people walk in and say, look, I need some help. They're kind of a decentralized approach to providing help for people, and that's very smart."

Page 10 paragraph 2

"But, unfortunately, there are loopholes in the program. Too much federal money is spent on things that have little to do with job training, such as management studies, or travel."

Page 10 paragraph 3

"Third, we need to require clear results of federal tax dollars that go to training workers. In other words, if we're going to spend $4 billion a year, we want to make sure we get results for the money. It's amazing what happens when you start to ask for results. The problem is there are now 17 different goals involved in the training programs. If you've got 17 goals, there really are no goals, right? I mean, if you've got so many goals, it's really hard to measure."

Page 11 paragraph 3

"We've got people from all walks of life who say, gosh, I'm stuck. I see the new jobs being created, but I don't have the skills necessary. This is an innovative world we live in, but I'm not—I don't have the skills necessary to be an innovative worker, and I want to improve myself. Where do I go? Where can I find help? Well, taxpayers' money is helping people do that. We just want to make sure the taxpayers' money we're spending is actually working to the maximum extent possible."

I read this speech and all I could think of was how much it is off the mark. The first part of the speech dealt with keeping jobs at home. To keep jobs at home, the United States Congress must pass class-action lawsuit reform, asbestos reform, for the sake of creating new jobs. Tort reform is necessary. Honestly, I was pretty lost about the asbestos reform. The opening part of this speech was extremely confusing.

In order to keep jobs at home, politicians should start working for the people who elected them. You can't get anything done in Washington because everybody is working on their campaign, getting contributions for their campaigns, or getting their strings pulled by some special interest group.

I don't know, maybe I completely missed the reference on how asbestos reform will help create jobs at home. Over the last 10 years we have let in millions of people into the country and have handed them American jobs. We have let American corporations use the Immigration and Naturalization Service as a job placement agency. I don't see the link to asbestos reform.

I actually read the speech about 5 times before I had to stop. Each time I read the speech, I had a tougher time connecting the dots. I could dissect each paragraph in this speech, but if you go through it a few times, I'm sure you will see what I mean.

President Bush Outlines Six Point Plan for the Economy
"A full agenda for the creation of jobs in America"
September 4, 2003

http://www.whitehouse.gov/news/releases/2003/09/20030904-3.html

Here we go, below is how we'll be rescued out of a mounting national debt, loss of millions of jobs, etc. It's going to be painful, but I'll wait until the end to comment on anything.

☐ **The President's Six Point Plan for the Economy**

☐ **Making Health Care Costs More Affordable and Predictable.** Health insurance costs for employers have been rising by 10 percent per year since 2000, causing businesses to hire fewer workers and too many families to go without insurance. President Bush proposes to allow small businesses to pool together to purchase health coverage for workers at lower rates; expand medical savings accounts to give workers more control over their health care insurance and costs; and reduce frivolous and excessive lawsuits against doctors and hospitals that drive up insurance costs for workers and businesses.

☐ **Reducing the Lawsuit Burden on Our Economy.** President Bush has proposed, and the House has approved, measures that would allow more class action and mass tort lawsuits to be moved into Federal court—so that trial lawyers have a harder time shopping for a favorable court. The President's reforms would also ensure that, in a class action lawsuit, most of the benefits of a settlement will actually go to the people who were injured. These reforms will help businesses focus on creating jobs, rather than fighting junk lawsuits.

☐ **Ensuring an Affordable, Reliable Energy Supply.** Businesses depend on affordable and reliable energy supplies. Energy shortages, price spikes, and blackouts disrupt the economy and discourage businesses from planning with confidence and adding new workers. President Bush has proposed a comprehensive national energy plan to upgrade the Nation's electrical grid, promote energy efficiency, increase domestic energy production, and provide enhanced conservation efforts, all while protecting the environment. It's time for Congress to finish its work and pass legislation based on the President's energy plan.

☐ **Streamlining Regulations and Reporting Requirements.** Government has a responsibility to ensure that its regulatory actions are reasonable and affordable. Too often, government regulations and compliance burdens discourage, rather than promote, job creation. The President will continue to work to simplify and streamline regulations, along with ensuring that well-intentioned compliance requirements do not have the unintended effect of killing jobs. The Administration also recently streamlined tax reporting requirements for small businesses, helping 2.6 million small businesses save 61 million hours of unproductive work.

☐ **Opening New Markets for American Products. American workers can compete with anyone in the world when given a chance.** Unfortunately, foreign taxes and tariffs drive up the costs of American products in too many countries, making our products more expensive and less competitive than those produced elsewhere. For example, in Chile, some kinds of American-made heavy machinery (such as motor graders) produced by American workers cost $11,200 more than those produced in the European Union or Canada solely because of tariffs. President Bush recently signed into law new free trade agreements with Chile and Singapore that will enable U.S. manufacturers to compete on a level playing field—and he will continue to work to open new markets to American products.

☐ **Enabling Families and Businesses to Plan for the Future with Confidence.** To make important spending, saving, and investment decisions, America's families and businesses need to be able to plan for the future. Right now, some key elements of the tax relief passed by Congress and signed into law by President Bush—such as the increase in the child tax credit, the elimination of the death tax, and the new incentives for small business investment—will expire in a few years. For example, a married couple with two children and an annual income of $40,000 would face a $922 tax increase (112percent increase) in 2005 if these and similar provisions in the Jobs and Growth Act are not made permanent. President Bush urges Congress to make these vital tax reductions permanent so America's families and businesses can make decisions for their financial futures.

☐ **These specific steps will help us build on our economic recovery and move on to the next stage of economic progress—the sustained expansion of employment.** The President looks forward to working with the Congress to pass a full agenda for the creation of jobs in America.

Reducing the Lawsuit Burden on the Economy—The President's reforms would also ensure that, in a class action lawsuit, most of the benefits of a settlement will actually go to the people who were injured. These reforms will help businesses focus on creating jobs, rather than fighting junk lawsuits. I don't know if I would include this in a plan to rescue the economy.

Ensuring an Affordable Reliable Energy Supply. If anyone has noticed the price of fuel goes up and down, up and down. The problem is that when it comes back down it never goes back to the old level or cheaper. It always lowers to a price that was higher than when it increased. We hear how this factor affected the price, but when they correct what made it go up they don't correct the price.

Between 1999 and 2000, when there was a change in the administration, the price of fuel was a little more than a dollar a gallon. What made the price jump over two dollars and fifty cents a gallon?

Less oil for a lot more money, I'm sure that it was painful to them to charge what they have been. We know how close of a relationship we have with these people, so the price will come down, at least until the election is over.

Streamlining Regulations and Reporting Requirements—too often government regulations and compliance burdens discourage, rather than promote jobs. If private companies were run the federal government, we would be in a major depression.

Opening new market for American products…in this point The President spoke about how some products costs $11,200 more than those produced in the European Union or Canada solely because of tariffs.

Enabling Families and Business to Plan for the Future with Confidence. All I have to say on this point is, you are giving all the jobs away. Americans are saving a lot less money now than they have in the last 5 years. It's survival now for many people, not planning for the future.

Our economy is finally beginning to rebound. It won't take long before you see people coming out of the woodwork trying to take credit for the improvement. These were probably the same people that were hiding for the last four years before it began to improve.

If you were looking at the speech made and the six point plan as an economist what would you think?

The American economy goes through corrections all the time. We have periods of growth and corrections. Everybody takes credit for the growth and blames everybody else for the corrections.

So what's the big difference between now and the past? We're now giving jobs away that should stay here. We're building economies for other nations instead of our own. High paying jobs are being farmed out and replaced with low paying jobs. And the list goes on………

Chapter 11
Happy Ending

So where does this all lead? Is there an end in sight to searching foreign countries for skilled labor?

You know when something is wrong and you can't put your finger on what it is exactly. I keep going back to the 2005 budget and thinking about a paragraph in there that just doesn't make sense. Why would you put in a budget, a paragraph stating that you are committed to reducing the backlog for foreign workers?

In the same paragraph, it states how the Administration is streamlining its permanent labor certification to help employers who cannot find domestic workers to fill specialized needs.

Wouldn't it be easier in your next speech to just say that you are willing to support the needs of big business and foreign countries by having the United States DOL become a placement agency?

Since the DOL also is moving to eliminate significant backlogs in employer applications filed under the old process, maybe you could have them do resumes for these people too. How about setting up some interviews with prospective employers. Maybe you could have a foreign job fair. That's actually not a bad idea. You could have all the companies set up booths and let them pick who they want to work for.

If this doesn't work out, maybe you could charge a user fee to Americans who are unemployed due to foreign labor. We could charge each American $500 dollars for becoming unemployed and use the money to help corporations find real skilled labor.

It all sounds so silly doesn't it? We talk about how we are so concerned about the job numbers and then we make it easier and easier for jobs to disappear.

During a recession, over a million jobs were taken by people coming in from the H-1B program. From 1999 to 2003 the number was capped at 195,000 people a year who were allowed in. Then in 2004, we reduced the number back to 65,000.

What country besides the United States would allow under one program, a million people to fill jobs during a recession? Remember, this is only under the H-1B program, this doesn't count all the other immigration programs.

Of course during an election year, jobs have become a hot topic. Many corporations are trying to distance themselves from the publicity that they are seeking foreign labor, so new companies are being set up to bring the people in under a different company name and then farm out the workers.

Everyday you hear that the economy is booming and those jobs are increasing by leaps and bounds. Then, you usually hear how the numbers were wrong, how they had to be adjusted, or how they didn't pick up as was initially expected.

I have seen first hand how the computer field has been destroyed. I watched people who went from earning $60-90K dollars a year to working in the local home improvement centers stocking shelves.

I have been involved in retraining workers who have permanently lost their jobs due to foreign labor and foreign manufacturing. I watched as they sold their homes and had to move back with their parents because they couldn't survive.

The computer field isn't the only area suffering; just about every field is now up for grabs.

Why would our elected officials fight so hard to pass immigration laws for foreign labor? They are fighting on behalf of foreign workers to create very favorable immigration laws.

I would like to pose a challenge to you—find out who is contributing to your elected officials who support visa legislation. You will have to do a little digging but I'm sure it would be worth it. Find out which PAC's (Political Action Committes), corporations, and groups are donating to your elected officials.

I'll bet you could go on the internet and find groups from certain countries who brag about how much money they donate. Not only that, look to see if they donate to both campaigns. They aren't stupid, they want to hedge their bet too.

Are these Senators and Congresspeople up for sale? Do you think in this country that it could be possible that campaign contributions could help influence a vote?

When I looked at some of the legislation being introduced, I wondered if some of these Senators or Congresspeople were here on H-1B visas. I wasn't sure which country some of them represented.

There are also many Senators and Congresspeople who fight hard to try to ensure that we aren't selling ourselves short. They know that not only are jobs at stake but the security of this nation. Unfortunately, the majority of our elected officials are passing legislation in favor of softer immigration laws.

In the Appendices of this book, I have included some of the resolutions from our elected officials regarding immigration and the legislation they are either trying or have passed. I included legislation that was both for and against some of these policies.

Our National debt is over $7 Trillion dollars and climbing. From the United States Treasury, I looked at the figures and it calculates it to the penny. By the time you actually look at the number, it has changed dramatically.

http://www.publicdebt.treas.gov/opd/opdpenny.htm

08/5/2004 $7,305,957,273,110.85

It's kind of strange that if a person started counting from the time they were born until they passed away that they could probably not count as high as a billion. Our national debt is in the trillions.

We can't afford to lose American jobs or industries. We have lost many jobs in the United States that has caused a permanent impact on our cities and states.

We need elected officials who are interested in the greater good of the American people and not their campaign. Our most important resource is our people.

As far as immigration and national security, we really need to pay attention. I don't mean getting up on a platform and dancing by telling us how safe we are, I mean actually correcting the problems.

One of my students who had been in high technology all his life said something to me that I could not forget. He told me as he got older; he looked forward to the golden years where he could finally retire. After being laid off and trying to find work, he said the only thing he had to look forward to was asking people if they wanted "Paper or Plastic".

I hope I never hear that again!

Appendix I
How Our Elected Officials Vote

When typing in the search, use the following key words—visas, immigration, and terrorism

http://thomas.loc.gov

Congressional Record article 2 of 50

FAILURE TO SOLVE H-2B VISA CRISIS—(Senate—May 04, 2004)
[Page: S4825]

Mr. LEAHY. Mr. President, I regret the need to once again call attention to the fact that the Senate continues to neglect our obligation to respond to a crisis, caused by Federal policy, that is disrupting the operations of small and large businesses throughout the United States.

Two months ago the Department of Homeland Security announced that for the first time ever the annual cap for H-2B visas had been met. A wide range of industries throughout the Nation to fill temporary labor needs uses these visas. In my home State of Vermont, they are used primarily by the tourist industry.

Across the country, businesses in a wide range of industries had developed plans that relied on the foreign employees who had always before been available to them. For years, these employers had applied in the spring for the employees they needed for the summer, filling positions for which they were unable to find American workers. The cap had never been reached, and they had no reason to believe this year would be different. I know that the March announcement came as a shock to many employers in my State, and dozens of them contacted my office to see what could be done. This setback fell equally hard on employers in other States.

In response to these requests, I joined with a substantial bipartisan coalition in introducing S. 2252, the Save Summer Act of 2004. Senator **KENNEDY** is the lead sponsor of the bill, which has 18 cosponsors, including eight Republicans. Our bill would add 40,000 visas for the current fiscal year, providing relief to those summer-oriented businesses that had never even had the opportunity to apply for visas.

The following day, Senator **HATCH** introduced S. 2258, the Summer Operations and Services Relief and Reform Act. I do not believe that this bill, cosponsored exclusively by

Republicans, is as effective a bill as S. 2252, but I would support it if it came before the Senate. Despite its sponsorship by the chairman of the Judiciary Committee, and by the chairman of the Immigration Subcommittee, S. 2258 has now been held hostage in the Republican cloakroom for 5 weeks.

Obtaining these visas takes weeks, if not months, because the Departments of Labor and Homeland Security must both sign off on them. Others and I have repeatedly warned that we needed to pass legislation by May 1 if we were going to provide meaningful relief. That date has come and gone, and now it is too late to help many, if not all, of the businesses that had relied upon the availability of H-2B visas. It is beyond disappointing that at the Republican leadership in this body ignored my pleas and the pleas of so many Senators. And it is inexcusable that the Republican leadership ignored the pleas of business owners across the country asking for this emergency relief.

And so it is that a tiny minority of the Republican caucus has managed to frustrate the will of a substantial bipartisan coalition of Senators who have sought to raise the H-2B cap, thereby needlessly harming businesses throughout the Nation. Meanwhile, the Republican leadership has failed to make solving this problem a priority. Perhaps if the majority leader chose to devote floor time to issues that had substantial bipartisan support, instead of using the floor to set up symbolic votes whose results are known well in advance, we would not be in this position.

These businesses contribute much to the economies of our States. They deserve better treatment than they have received at the hands of the Republican leadership of the Senate.

Congressional Record article 8 of 50

H-2B VISA CRISIS—(Senate—May 21, 2004)
[Page: S6083]

Mr. JEFFORDS. Mr. President, today I would like to discuss my disappointment with the failure to address an issue of critical importance to small businesses around the country—the need to consider legislation temporarily raising the cap on the number of H-2B visas for this fiscal year.

As many of my colleagues know after hearing from their constituents, the limit on the number of H-2B visas that could be issued this fiscal year was reached in early March. The H-2B cap was reached less than halfway through the current fiscal year and has caused critical problems around the country. This is especially true for those small businesses that rely on H-2B visas to completely fill their staffing needs over the summer months. A business may apply for a H-2B visa no sooner than 120 days before the individual is needed for employment, and the cap was reached as businesses were applying for their summer positions.

I quickly heard from many Vermont businesses expressing their concerns about not being able to obtain these needed workers, and I was pleased to join Senator *Kennedy* in introducing the Save the Summer Act on March 29, 2004. This commonsense approach would raise the cap on H-2B visas for this fiscal year by 40,000. This is a simple, straight-forward, easy-to-understand-and-implement solution to this problem. I was pleased that the bill had bipartisan support when it was introduced and I was hopeful that it could be considered and passed quickly in the Senate. Unfortunately, this was not to be the case.

The next day, on March 30, Senator *Hatch* introduced the Summer Operations and Services Relief and Reform Act that addressed the H-2B cap problem in a different manner. While I felt that this legislation addressed the problem in a less clear, more complicated way, I was very pleased that the Senate Judiciary Committee chairman, Senator *Hatch*, and the Judiciary Committee's Immigration Subcommittee chairman, Senator *Chambliss*, recognized that there was a problem that had to be immediately addressed.

In the normal legislative process, the next step should have been for the two sides to sit down and try to work through the differences between the bills and then quickly pass legislation to solve this problem. However, in this case, the Republicans on the Senate Judiciary Committee were not in agreement on how to address the matter and began to negotiate among themselves. Unfortunately, they chose not to negotiate with the supporters of the Save the Summer Act until they had reached a consensus. Supposedly, more than a month after the bill was introduced, the Republicans finally reached an agreement amongst themselves.

Although the majority reached a consensus, the business community and the Department of Homeland Security raised concerns about the Republican agreement.

Thus, the Republicans have gone back to the drawing board and are once again negotiating amongst themselves.

It is now the day before the Senate will take its break for the Memorial Day holiday. Many think of Memorial Day weekend as the unofficial beginning of summer. However, almost 2 months after legislation had been introduced, businesses around the country that were counting on the Congress to solve this problem still do not have an answer. Summer may have begun, but for many businesses, this summer season will not be something to celebrate.

Senator *Kennedy* and I introduced a simple, easy solution to this problem on March 29 that would have allowed businesses to obtain the employees they desperately need for the summer, while giving the Congress the opportunity to address the long-term issues with the H2-B program. However, the Republican leadership will not allow the Senate to pass this legislation with an overwhelming vote.

It has been almost 2 months since legislation was introduced, almost 3 months since the problem arose, and the Republicans are still debating the issue internally. The Senate should pass the Save the Summer Act immediately and help our Nation's small businesses.

Congressional Record article 9 of 50

NATIONAL SECURITY THREAT, FRAUD AND ABUSE ASSOCIATED WITH VISA LOTTERY PROGRAM—(House of Representatives—June 22, 2004)
[Page: H4730]

The SPEAKER pro tempore. Under a previous order of the House, the gentleman from Virginia (Mr. *Goodlatte*) is recognized for 5 minutes.

Mr. GOODLATTE. Mr. Speaker, I rise today to discuss a government program that presents a serious national security threat and is wrought with fraud and abuse, the visa lottery program.

Under the program, each successful applicant is chosen at random and given the status of permanent resident, a green card holder, based on pure luck. A perfect example of the system gone awry is the case of Hesham Mohamed Ali Hedayet, the Egyptian national who killed two and wounded three during a shooting spree at the Los Angeles International Airport in July of 2002. He was allowed to apply for lawful permanent resident status in 1997 because of his wife's status as a visa lottery winner.

The State Department's Inspector General has even weighed in on the national security threat posed by the visa lottery program. In a report issued in September of 2003, the Office of Inspector General stated that the visa lottery program contains "significant threats to national security from entry of hostile intelligence officers, criminals, and terrorists into the United States as permanent residents."

Usually immigrant visas are issued to foreign nationals who have existing connections with family members lawfully residing in the United States. These types of relationships help ensure that immigrants entering our country have a stake in continuing America's success and have needed skills to contribute to our Nation's economy. However, under the visa lottery program, visas are awarded to immigrants at random without meeting such criteria.

In addition, the visa lottery program is unfair to immigrants who comply with the United States' immigration laws. The visa lottery program does not expressly prohibit illegal immigrants from applying to receive visas through the program. Thus the program treats foreign nationals that comply with our laws the same as those that blatantly violate our laws. In addition, most family-sponsored immigrants currently face a wait of years to obtain visas. Yet the lottery program pushes 50,000 random immigrants with no particular family ties, job skills, or education ahead of these families and employer-sponsored immigrants each year with relatively no wait. This sends the wrong message to those who wish to enter our great country and to the international community as a whole.

Furthermore, the visa lottery program is wrought with fraud. A recent report released by the Center for Immigration Studies states that it is commonplace for foreign nationals to apply for the lottery program multiple times using many different aliases. In addition, the visa lottery program has spawned a cottage industry featuring sponsors in the U.S. who falsely promise success to applicants in exchange for large sums of money. Ill-informed foreign nationals are willing to pay top dollar for the "guarantee" of lawful permanent resident status in the U.S.

The State Department's Office of Inspector General confirms these allegations of widespread fraud in its September report. Specifically, the report states that the visa lottery program is "subject to widespread abuse" and that "identity fraud is endemic and fraudulent documents are commonplace." Furthermore, the report also reveals that the State Department found that 364,000 duplicate applications were detected in 2003 alone. The only penalty for such abuse is disqualification from that year's lottery.

The visa lottery program represents what is wrong with our country's immigration system. The serious national security threats, fraud, and waste that the visa lottery program present begs the question: Why is this program still in existence?

Last February I introduced H.R. 775, the Security and Fairness Enhancement, or SAFE, for America Act.

[Time: 18:00]

This important legislation would eliminate the controversial visa lottery program. Not only will the removal of the visa lottery improve our Nation's security but it will also make the administration of our immigration laws more consistent and fair and help reduce immigration fraud and opportunism.

I urge each of my colleagues to support this important legislation.

Congressional Record article 13 of 50

AMENDING THE IMMIGRATION AND NATIONALITY ACT—(Senate—October 03, 2003)

[Page: S12477]

Mr. FRIST. Mr. President, I ask unanimous consent that the Judiciary Committee be discharged from further consideration of H.R. 2152, and the Senate proceed to its immediate consideration.

The PRESIDING OFFICER. Without objection, it is so ordered. The clerk will report the bill by title.

The assistant legislative clerk read as follows:

A bill (H.R. 2152) to amend the immigration and nationality act to extend for an additional 5 years the special immigrant religious worker program.

There being no objection, the Senate proceeded to consider the bill.

Mr. LEAHY. Mr. President, this House bill is identical to S. 1580, the Religious Workers Act of 2003, of which I am a proud cosponsor. The bill extends for 5 years provisions of our immigration law that provide for special immigrant visas for religious workers sponsored by religious organizations in the United States. These visas allow religious denominations or organizations in the United States to bring in foreign nationals to perform religious work here. This modest program—which provides for up to 5,000 religious immigrant visas a year—was created in the Immigration Act of 1990, and has been extended ever since.

These religious workers contribute significantly not just to their religious communities, but also to the community as a whole. They work in hospitals, nursing homes, and homeless shelters. They help immigrants and refugees adjust to the United States. In other words, they perform vital tasks that all too often go undone.

I have worked on this issue over the years, and cosponsored bills in 1997 and 2000 that would have made this program permanent. I still believe that it should be permanent but fully support a 5-year extension as the next best thing. Time is now of the essence as we have entered FY 2004 and allowed this program to lapse.

The House passed this bill last month by voice vote. I urge the Senate to follow suit by approving this extension and sending it to the President without further delay.

Mr. FRIST. I ask unanimous consent the bill be read a third time and passed, the motion to reconsider be laid upon the table, and any statements relating to the bill be printed in the **RECORD**.

The PRESIDING OFFICER. Without objection, it is so ordered.

The bill (H.R. 2152) was read the third time and passed.

Congressional Record article 18 of 50

SUPPORTING THE IMMIGRANT WORKERS FREEDOM RIDE—HON. JOE BACA (Extensions of Remarks—October 02, 2003)

[Page: E1965]

HON. JOE BACA
OF CALIFORNIA
IN THE HOUSE OF REPRESENTATIVES
Thursday, October 2, 2003

- Mr. BACA. Mr. Speaker, I rise to give tribute to the Immigrant Freedom Ride. These immigrants have crossed the country to ask Congress to allow them a process for naturalization, increase the number of visas for family reunification, and to protect the civil and labor rights of immigrants.

- Immigrants need a process to earn legal status. These immigrants work hard, pay taxes, and want to be productive legal members of our society.

- Many immigrants live in solitude. Work and send their money home so that their children and families can survive. That is why immigrants need more visas so we can reunite families. No parent should be forced out of necessity to miss out on the life of his or her child.

- And, we must protect the civil rights of all immigrants—including the undocumented. Too many immigrant workers are fired if they speak up about labor violations. Labor protections should apply to all workers, not just citizens. These demands are just.

- Immigrants break their backs picking our fruits and vegetables, building our homes, and making our clothes. But, they will no longer be silent. They demand fair treatment.

- This is a wakeup call. Immigrants are angry and will not be silent anymore.

- I support the ideals of the Immigrant Freedom Ride and aim to help immigrants achieve these goals.

Congressional Record article 20 of 50

IN SUPPORT OF H.R. 775—(Extensions of Remarks—May 21, 2004)

[Page: E956]

SPEECH OF
HON. MARSHA BLACKBURN
OF TENNESSEE
IN THE HOUSE OF REPRESENTATIVES
THURSDAY, MAY 20, 2004

- Mrs. BLACKBURN. Mr. Speaker, many of our immigration laws are no longer consistent with our national security and other vital interests.

- The diversity visa or visa lottery system is one such example. The visa lottery was established by the Immigration Act of 1990 to offer the opportunity of immigration to individuals in countries that had been sending few immigrants to the United States.

- Usually, immigrant visas are issued to foreign nationals that have an existing connection with a family member lawfully residing in the United States or with a U.S. employer. These types of relationships help ensure that immigrants entering the country have a stake in continuing America's success, and have the advanced skills necessary to contribute to the nation's economy. However, under the visa lottery program, visas are awarded to immigrants at random with no such safety precautions.

- I have heard from immigrants who have legally come to the country, and they believe the visa lottery program is unfair to immigrants who comply with the United States' immigration laws. Also, the visa lottery program does not prohibit illegal immigrants from applying to receive a visa through the program.

- The program has many flaws. A recent report released by the Center for Immigration Studies shows that it is commonplace for foreign nationals to apply for the lottery program multiple times using different aliases and false personal information.

- I support Congressman Goodlatte's bill, H.R. 775, The Security and Fairness Enhancement for America Act, which would terminate the visa lottery. This piece of legislation is an important and positive step in immigration reform and it is my hope that the House considers it in the near future.

Congressional Record article 22 of 50

THE INTRODUCTION OF THE COMPASSIONATE VISITOR VISA ACT TO FACILITATE THE TEMPORARY ADMISSION OF NONIMMIGRANT IMMI-GRANTS IN CIRCUMSTANCES OF FAMILY EMERGENCY OF CITIZENS OR PERMANENT RESIDENTS—(House of Representatives—October 16, 2003)
[Page: H9608]

The SPEAKER pro tempore. Under a previous order of the House, the gentleman from Hawaii (Mr. *Case*) is recognized for 5 minutes.

Mr. CASE. Madam Speaker, I rise today to introduce the compassionate Visitor Visa Act, a bill to facilitate the temporary admission into our country of nonimmigrant immigrants, who present no security risk, in times of family emergency for close relatives that are United States citizens or legal permanent residents.

Mr. Speaker, each of us tries to make the best decisions we can on the national and international issues of our day. But each of us is also committed to helping those we serve with their individual concerns, where the rubber of our national policies meets the road of everyday life. And those of us who represent communities of proud immigrants maintaining close ties to their homelands know that a large, growing, and increasingly difficult and frustrating portion of our casework is devoted to immigration.

In my own case, these issues involve citizens and legal residents with ties to the countries of Asia and the Pacific, the Philippines foremost among them (my district has more Filipino-Americans than any other congressional district in our country.) And of the related immigration concerns my constituents have sought my assistance with, none have been more difficult and heart wrenching than those involving the efforts of families to be reunited in time of family emergency.

Consider the following real-life examples from my own district experience:

A U.S. citizen mother was diagnosed with a terminal illness. She wanted to see her daughter, a Philippine citizen, from whom she had been separated for 15 years, one last time. Her daughter had remained in the Philippines by choice with her husband and children when the rest of the family emigrated to the U.S. She had no desire to emigrate and was willing to travel to see her dying mother without her husband and children. Nonetheless, she was denied a temporary nonimmigrant visa to say a final farewell and to attend her mother's funeral because she was not able to demonstrate affirmatively that she would in fact return to the Philippines.

A terminally ill U.S. citizen had not seen any of her siblings for more than 20 years and wanted to see just one of them one last time. Her sister applied for a nonimmigrant visa to be able to visit and care for her sibling in her final days. Similarly, she was going to leave her own husband and young children behind in the Philippines. Her visa application was denied, the reason cited being that because her husband's income was modest and she was not employed, the assumption was the she would not return to the Philippines.

Madam Speaker, these are compelling stories of a well-intentioned immigration policy gone very wrong.

Let me first say that the problem these stories graphically illustrate and the solution my bill offers have nothing to do with preserving our homeland security. The reason for the rejection of these applicants was in no way related to any assessment of their security risk. They were subject to a security review like other applicants, and nothing in the compassionate Visa Act would alter that. All of that stands as it is and as it should be. (I will comment that resources to process security reviews in a timely and efficient manner are woefully inadequate to meet demand, but that is another discussion.)

The reason lies instead in the application of the presumption clause in current immigration law. In practice, applicants for nonimmigrant visas are presumed to be at risk of defaulting on their visas and remaining in our country illegally unless they can affirmatively prove that they will return to their countries. In the cases above, the applicants provided documentation to overcome this presumption and demonstrate they had every reason to return to their country of origin: they maintained homes, businesses, bank accounts, and would leave other family members, often children, behind, but to no avail.

We can and should have an in-depth debate about whether this policy, in theory and practice, is wise or fair across-the-board as to all nonimmigrant visa applicants, but this bill does not engage in that larger picture. What the Compassionate Visa Act does say, however, is that the presumption clause, as applied to close family members, who are not security risks, of U.S. citizens or legal permanent residents that are seriously ill or who have died, is wrong and should be changed.

Opponents of the bill may argue that the results would be to detract from homeland security and enhance the default rate on nonimmigrant visas. First, for the third time, nothing in this bill changes or compromises procedures designed to identify and weed out security threats, so that cannot be used as an excuse to avoid the focus of this bill. Second, this bill does not say that consular officers cannot consider evidence of applicants' willingness to honor visa terms and return to their countries, but it does say that the deck won't be virtually impossibly stacked against them from the get-go. And third, this bill applies only in the narrow case of an applicant whose close family member has a serious illness or has died or has some other similar family emergency, as demonstrated by proof to the satisfaction of the immigration officers. Frankly, I don't accept that changing the presumption clause will increase the default rate.

Madam Speaker, this is the right thing to do, and we should do it.

Congressional Record article 26 of 50

EXTENDING THE DURATION OF THE IMMIGRANT INVESTOR REGIONAL CENTER PILOT PROGRAM—(Senate—October 03, 2003)

[Page: S12476]

Mr. FRIST. I ask unanimous consent that the Judiciary Committee be discharged from further consideration of S. 1642, and that the Senate proceed to its immediate consideration.

The PRESIDING OFFICER. Without objection it is so ordered. The clerk will report the bill by title.

The assistant legislative clerk read as follows:

A bill (S. 1642) to extend the duration of the immigrant investor regional center pilot program for 5 additional years, and for other purposes.

There being no objection, the Senate proceeded to consider the bill.

Mr. LEAHY. Mr. President, I urge the Senate to pass S. 1642, a bill to extend for 5 years the EB-5 immigrant investor visa regional center pilot program, which lapsed at the end of the fiscal year on Tuesday. I am pleased that Senators BROWNBACK and DASCHLE have joined me in sponsoring this bill. There are more than 25 regions in the Nation that have qualified as a "regional center" under this program, including in my State of Vermont. This designation allows them to attract foreign investment by adjusting the standard that investors must meet to obtain legal permanent resident status. The entrepreneurs must still meet a heavy burden, however, showing that their investment will create 10 or more jobs in these relatively depressed areas.

The pilot program is narrowly tailored to avoid fraud. An area seeking regional center status must provide, among other things, detailed information regarding how the center will promote economic growth through improved regional productivity, job creation, and increased domestic capital investment. The applicant must also provide a detailed explanation of why the regional center will have a positive impact on the regional or national economy in general.

The Judiciary Committee approved the language in this bill unanimously, as part of a substitute amendment to S. 1580, the Religious Workers Act of 2003. I am pleased to include an amendment from Senator FEINGOLD that the Judiciary Committee also unanimously approved, calling for a GAO study on the EB-5 program as a whole. Such a study will give us a better idea of how the program is working and what improvements may be needed.

This is an important program for my State and many other regions of the country, and I ask for the support of all Senators in extending it for an additional 5 years.

Mr. FRIST. I ask unanimous consent that the Feingold amendment, which is at the desk, be considered, agreed to, the bill as amended be read three times and passed, the motion to reconsider be laid upon the table with no intervening action or debate, and that any statements related to the bill be printed in the RECORD.

The PRESIDING OFFICER. Without objection, it is so ordered.

The amendment (No. 1827) was agreed to, as follows:

AMENDMENT NO. 1827

(Purpose: To require the General Accounting Office to report to Congress on the immigrant investor program)

At the end, add the following:

SEC. 2. GAO STUDY.

(a) **IN GENERAL.**—Not later than 1 year after the date of enactment of this Act, the General Accounting Office shall report to Congress on the immigrant investor program created under section 203(b)(5) of the Immigration and Nationality Act (8 U.S.C. 1153(b)(5)).

(b) **CONTENTS.**—The report described in subsection (a) shall include information regarding—

(1) the number of immigrant investors that have received visas under the immigrant investor program in each year since the inception of the program;

(2) the country of origin of the immigrant investors;

(3) the localities where the immigrant investors are settling and whether those investors generally remain in the localities where they initially settle;

(4) the number of immigrant investors that have sought to become citizens of the United States;

(5) the types of commercial enterprises that the immigrant investors have established; and

(6) the types and number of jobs created by the immigrant investors.

The bill (S. 1642), as amended, was read the third time and passed, as follows:

S. 1642

Be it enacted by the Senate and House of Representatives of the United States of America in Congress assembled,

SECTION 1. PILOT IMMIGRATION PROGRAM.

(a) **PROCESSING PRIORITY UNDER PILOT IMMIGRATION PROGRAM FOR REGIONAL CENTERS TO PROMOTE ECONOMIC GROWTH.**—Section 610 of the Departments of Commerce, Justice, and State, the Judiciary, and Related Agencies Appropriations Act, 1993 (8 U.S.C. 1153 note) is amended—

[Page: S12477]

(1) by striking "Attorney General" each place such term appears and inserting "Secretary of Homeland Security"; and

(2) by adding at the end the following:

"(d) In processing petitions under section 204(a)(1)(H) of the Immigration and Nationality Act (8 U.S.C. 1154(a)(1)(H)) for classification under section 203(b)(5) of such Act (8 U.S.C. 1153(b)(5)), the Secretary of Homeland Security may give priority to petitions filed by immigrants seeking admission under the pilot program described in this section. Notwithstanding section 203(e) of such Act (8 U.S.C. 1153(e)), immigrant visas made available under such section 203(b)(5) may be issued to such immigrants in an order that takes into account any priority accorded under the preceding sentence.".

(b) **EXTENSION.**—Section 610(b) of the Departments of Commerce, Justice, and State, the Judiciary, and Related Agencies Appropriations Act, 1993 (8 U.S.C. 1153 note) is amended by striking "10 years" and inserting "15 years".

SEC. 2. GAO STUDY.

(a) **IN GENERAL.**—Not later than 1 year after the date of enactment of this Act, the General Accounting Office shall report to Congress on the immigrant investor program created under section 203(b)(5) of the Immigration and Nationality Act (8 U.S.C. 1153(b)(5)).

(b) **CONTENTS.**—The report described in subsection (a) shall include information regarding—

(1) the number of immigrant investors that have received visas under the immigrant investor program in each year since the inception of the program;

(2) the country of origin of the immigrant investors;

(3) the localities where the immigrant investors are settling and whether those investors generally remain in the localities where they initially settle;

(4) the number of immigrant investors that have sought to become citizens of the United States;

(5) the types of commercial enterprises that the immigrant investors have established; and

(6) the types and number of jobs created by the immigrant investors.

Congressional Record article 30 of 50

MESSAGE FROM THE SENATE—(House of Representatives—March 24, 2003)
[Page: H2273]

A message from the Senate by Mr. Monahan, one of its clerks, announced that the Senate has passed a bill of the following title in which the concurrence of the House is requested:

S. 205. An act to authorize the issuance of immigrant visas to, and the admission to the United States for permanent residence of, certain scientists, engineers, and technicians who have worked in Iraqi weapons of mass destruction programs.

Congressional Record article 37 of 50

FRENCH VISAS TO THE IRAQI REGIME—(House of Representatives—May 07, 2003)

[Page: H3686]

(Mr. PITTS asked and was given permission to address the House for 1 minute and to revise and extend his remarks.)

Mr. PITTS. Mr. Speaker, right after September 11, France voiced its support in the war on terrorism. Lately, we are hearing a different story. It has been reported that the French Government secretly supplied fleeing Iraqi officials with passports in Syria to allow them to escape to Europe. The French passports allowed the wanted Iraqis to move freely among 12 European Union countries.

There are also reports indicating that a French company covertly sold spare military parts to Iraq in the weeks before the war and that a French oil company was working with a Russian oil firm to conclude a deal with Saddam's government in the days before military action began March 19.

All of this has undermined our efforts to root out terrorists in Iraq and capture members of the brutal Iraqi regime. If France wants to be an ally in the war on terrorism, it is time it started to act like one.

Congressional Record article 39 of 50

REPORTS OF COMMITTEES—(Senate—January 30, 2003)
[Page: S1811]

The following reports of committees were submitted:

By Mr. SHELBY, without amendment:

S. Res. 35. An original resolution authorizing expenditures by the Committee on Banking, Housing, and Urban Affairs.

By Mr. DOMENICI, without amendment:

S. Res. 36. An original resolution authorizing expenditures by the Committee on Energy and Natural Resources.

By Mr. McCAIN, without amendment:

S. Res. 37. An original resolution authorizing expenditures by the Committee on Commerce, Science, and Transportation.

By Mr. CRAIG, without amendment:

S. Res. 38. An original resolution authorizing expenditures by the Special Committee on Aging.

By Mr. GREGG, without amendment:

S. Res. 39. An original resolution authorizing expenditures by the Committee on Health, Education, Labor, and Pensions.

By Mr. HATCH, from the Committee on the Judiciary, with amendments:

S. 151. A bill to amend title 18, United States Code, with respect to the sexual exploitation of children.

By Mr. HATCH, from the Committee on the Judiciary, without amendment:

S. 153. A bill to amend title 18, United States Code, to establish penalties for aggravated identity theft, and for other purposes.

S. 205. A bill to authorize the issuance of immigrant visas to, and the admission to the United States for permanent residence of, certain scientists, engineers, and technicians who have worked in Iraqi weapons of mass destruction programs.

Congressional Record article 45 of 50 (Partial Record)

STATEMENTS ON INTRODUCED BILLS AND JOINT RESOLUTIONS— (Senate—March 29, 2004)

[Page: S3296]

By Ms. COLLINS (for herself and Mr. LIEBERMAN):

S. 2249. A bill to amend the Stewart B. McKinney Homeless Assistance Act to provide for emergency food and shelter; to the Committee on Governmental Affairs.

Ms. COLLINS. Mr. President, I rise today to introduce legislation to reauthorize the Department of Homeland Security's Emergency Food and Shelter Program. This vital program enables communities nationwide to provide services to help individuals who are at risk of becoming homeless or going hungry due to an emergency or economic disaster. As a 1999 General Accounting Office report concluded, "in most areas of the United States, the Emergency Food and Shelter Program is the only source of funding for the prevention of homelessness."

I am pleased to have the support of Senator LIEBERMAN, the ranking member of the Governmental Affairs Committee, which oversees this important program as well as the Department of Homeland Security generally. I commend Senator LIEBERMAN for his work on this important issue, including his efforts in the 107th Congress to pass legislation very similar to the bill that we are introducing together today.

Since its creation 21 years ago, the Emergency Food and Shelter Program has provided a helping hand to local social service organizations that assist thousands of people in need of food and shelter. This program is effective because of the way it is structured. A national board, chaired by the Federal Emergency Management Agency, governs the program. The board itself is composed of representatives from organizations who work every day to look out for those who are less fortunate—representatives of the American Red Cross, Catholic Charities, United Jewish Communities, the National Council of the Churches, the Salvation Army, and the United Way.

This program is a model for an effective public-private partnership. The volunteer participation by these charitable organizations has kept administrative costs to less than 3 percent of the total program, making even more funds directly available for communities.

Funds are distributed by the national board to local boards according to a formula that takes into account unemployment and poverty statistics in each community. Once local boards in counties and municipalities across America receive the funding, they decide how to best address the needs of their residents. These local boards are key to this process. That is because they are composed of individuals and organizations that live and work in the communities they serve. Therefore, they can best decide how to meet the needs of those who are at risk of becoming homeless.

In recent years, communities in Maine have put the funding to good use. Communities in Cumberland and Franklin Counties, for example, have used most of these funds to supplement the efforts of local soup kitchens, Meals-on Wheels programs, and food pantries. The Wayside Soup Kitchen in Portland, ME, uses this funding to enhance their efforts to provide three separate food assistance programs to those in need.

Demonstrating the flexibility of this program, communities in northern Maine's

Aroostook County used more than 30 percent of their 2003 funding to address emergency shelter and housing needs. This diversity in how communities spent these funds highlights the importance of letting local organizations decide how best to spend these resources, tailored to local needs.

The Emergency Food and Shelter Program helps individuals maintain their dignity during difficult times. It also prevents dependency by providing emergency services to individuals and families on a limited basis so they can remain self-sufficient.

Although Congress has continued to provide funding, the program's authorization expired in 1994. My bill, the Emergency Food and Shelter Act of 2004, seeks to again authorize this program and provide modest increases to reflect an increasing need.

I urge my colleagues to join me in cosponsoring this legislation to help families across America who are at risk of losing their homes or going hungry because of circumstances beyond their control.

By Mr. *KENNEDY* (for himself, Ms. *Snowe*, Mr. *Leahy*, Mr. *Gregg*, Mr. *Jeffords*, Ms. *Murkowski*, Mr. *Sarbanes*, Ms. *Collins*, Mrs. *Murray*, Mr. *Stevens*, Mr. *Edwards*, Mr. *McCain*, Mr. *Daschle*, Mr. *Sununu*, and Mr. *Enzi*):

S. 2252. A bill to increase the number of immigrants who may receive certain nonimmigrant status during fiscal year 2004 and to require submissions of information by the Secretary of Homeland Security; to the Committee on the Judiciary.

Mr. KENNEDY. It is a privilege to join my colleagues in introducing the Save Summer Act of 2004 to provide an immediate stopgap solution to the H-2B visa cap problem in our immigration laws. Our colleagues, Representatives *Delahunt* and *Young*, are introducing an identical bill in the House.

Congress established the H-2B program in 1990 to deal with labor shortages in nonagricultural seasonal employment. Hotels, restaurants, resorts, the fishing and timber industries, amusement parks, and other sectors employ H-2B workers.

U.S. employers seeking to bring in foreign nationals on these visas must demonstrate that they have been unable to find enough U.S. workers to fill

[Page: S3297]

the jobs. Before visa applications are approved by the Department of Labor, the U.S. employers must certify that the temporary workers will not displace U.S. workers or adversely affect their wages or working conditions.

The annual statutory cap for H-2B visas is 66,000. Two weeks ago, the Department of Homeland Security suddenly announced that the cap for the current fiscal year had been reached and began rejecting new applications for the visas. The abrupt announcement left many summer employers stranded. This is the first time the Government has announced that the cap has been reached, and the Department of Homeland Security gave no one advance warning.

The H-2B program is vital for seasonal industries that need temporary workers. The lack of H-2B workers may well be devastating to these employers, many of which are small, family-run businesses. Without prompt passage of this bill, many summer employers in Massachusetts and around the country will have no choice but to shut their doors.

The Save the Summer Act offers a straightforward solution to this pressing problem. It will increase the H-2B visa cap by 40,000 for the current fiscal year. It requires the Department of Homeland Security to provide quarterly reports to Congress on the number of H-2B visas issued, and an annual report with a detailed analysis of the program.

Our immigration system is broken and many other reforms are obviously needed. Above all, it is essential to have immigration policies that reflect current economic realities, respect family unity and fundamental fairness, and uphold our proud tradition as a Nation of immigrants.

Enacting these other reforms will take time—time we don't have if we want to save the summer for countless seasonal employers around the country. This legislation will provide immediate and much-needed relief to employers counting on H-2B workers to keep their doors open this summer, and I urge my colleagues to pass it as soon as possible.

Congressional Record article 49 of 50

IMMIGRATION POLICY—(Extensions of Remarks—May 19, 2004)

[Page: E909]

SPEECH OF
HON. STEVE KING
OF IOWA
IN THE HOUSE OF REPRESENTATIVES
WEDNESDAY, MAY 19, 2004

- Mr. KING of Iowa. Mr. Speaker, I wholly support an immigration policy designed to enhance the economic, social and cultural well-being of the United States of America. I am looking forward to working on immigration policy as a member of the Subcommittee on Immigration, Border Security, and Claims. I intend to carry out the responsibility for crafting the immigration and naturalization policy that was delegated to Congress by our Constitution.

- Immigrants have made, and will continue to make, a valuable contribution to our Nation. I will work to develop an immigration policy that aids in the assimilation of newcomers by ensuring that the United States does not admit more immigrants than it can reasonably accommodate. Assimilation is valuable to immigrants who benefit from our shared American culture of personal responsibility, freedom and patriotism. The values shared by our civilization, founded on a heritage of western civilization, religious freedom and free enterprise capitalism, serve immigrants and native born alike. I am concerned that the recent rise in immigration levels in this country will make it difficult for newcomers to assimilate and find jobs. We must ensure cultural continuity for our great Nation.

- As Americans, we should promote a naturalization process that promotes American values, the responsibilities of citizenship and our constitutional principles. We must be careful to admit only as many newcomers as we can accommodate with jobs so that our society will not be burdened by unemployed immigrants.

- Candidates for naturalization should be proficient in the English language. Not only will English proficiency help newcomers attain better paying jobs, it also provides a means of communication with all Americans. For this reason, I have recently introduced the English Language Unity Act of 2003, H.R. 997 to declare English the official language of the United States.

- Finally, as a sovereign nation, we must control our borders. We must ensure that terrorists do not infiltrate the United States. We must tighten and strengthen border control efforts so that illegal immigrants do not enter our country. I support elimination of the visa lottery which gives randomly selected individuals visas, when many law abiding would-be immigrants are waiting to have their applications approved. I am also concerned about the enforcement of immigration laws within our borders.

- I hope that this Congress will be vigilant in our oversight of the enforcement of existing immigration laws and make necessary changes to existing laws.

Appendix II
Do You Really Want to Know

When typing in the search, use the following key words—visas, immigration, terrorism

http://thomas.loc.gov

Congressional Record article 1 of 50

REFORM OUR OUTDATED IMMIGRATION LAWS AND POLICIES—
(Extensions of Remarks—May 21, 2004)

[Page: E958]

SPEECH OF
HON. BRAD CARSON
OF OKLAHOMA
IN THE HOUSE OF REPRESENTATIVES
THURSDAY, MAY 20, 2004

- Mr. CARSON of Oklahoma. Mr. Speaker, I rise today to urge that Congress make it a top priority to reform our outdated immigration laws and policies.

- The tragic events of September 11th awakened most Americans to the fact that our immigration system is seriously flawed and overwhelmed by the massive numbers of foreign visitors and immigrants flowing through it into our country. We all saw then that immigration policy has serious national security impacts and weaknesses. Since that time, Congress and the Executive Branch have made a number of statutory, regulatory and policy changes that have addressed from a homeland security perspective some of the many systemic flaws in thus immigration process. Of course, a great deal remains to be done to ensure appropriate levels of safety for America.

- We still have 12 to 15 million, or even more, foreign immigrants living and working here illegally. Fortunately, most are not security threats and are simply seeking to improve their economic status by working here where they can make much more than in their home countries. But, undoubtedly some number are here to do us harm either as terrorists, or, more likely, by engaging in criminal activities. We must continue working to identify and expel those who pose such public safety threats.

- We also must address the fundamental issue of reducing the extraordinary immigration numbers that we are experiencing year after year. I believe that immigration is a good thing, and most immigrants are good people, here seeking the American Dream. However, I have no doubt that the extremely high numbers of legal and illegal immigrants we have been allowing to come here in recent years represent "too much of a good thing"—numbers matter, and simply put, our immigration numbers, two-thirds of which are due to legal admissions, are excessive. This is especially so given the changing nature of America's labor markets, where low-skilled workers find their jobs disappearing or wages stagnating. Our labor market clearly does not need the roughly 1 1/2 million new immigrants who move to the United States every year. Inordinately high numbers of immigrants, most of whom are less educated and relatively low skilled are having real, and often adverse, impacts on American life.

- Citizens and earlier immigrants, who often remain lower skilled and less educated, are suffering serious job and wage losses due to the continuing massive cheap foreign labor inflows. Such problems would be greatly lessened if we reduce both legal and illegal immigration to more moderate and sustainable levels. Congress today has the power to do so, by reviewing legal immigration policy and by genuinely enforcing a policy against illegal immigration.

- We have been experiencing such a large immigrant inflow now for several decades due both to lax enforcement and more importantly to statutory changes made in the 1980s and 1990s that opened the immigration floodgates to an unprecedented degree. Congress essentially reset the immigration thermostat and forgot about it, despite the increasingly obvious and serious impacts this has been having.

- Congress can no longer ignore the immigration numbers issue. In addition to ensuring better enforcement of our laws so as to radically curtail illegal inflows, we must readjust legal admission policies to ensure that legal immigration fits the reality of America's 21st century labor market. It has been recognized for years by those who have bothered to examine how our current system works that statutory changes are needed to eliminate a number of unnecessary admission categories. For example, the Immigration Reform Commission, chaired by the late Rep. Barbara Jordan, recommended repealing the visa lottery, which allows thousands of people to come here merely because their name was drawn in a lottery, and the extended family visa categories which spawn literally endless chain migration.

- For starters, I believe that we need to reduce legal admission numbers by ending the visa lottery and the so-called extended family categories that fuel foreign worker inflow by chain migration. A positive first step at reforming our outdated immigration laws would be to pass H.R. 775, the Goodlatte bill that repeals the visa lottery. As a cosponsor of that bill, I urge the House Leadership and the Judiciary Committee to act to bring the bill before the full House for action, and to advance other legislation to ensure that our legal immigration policy, coupled with our blind eye toward illegal immigration, are reviewed.

Congressional Record article 2 of 50

IMMIGRATION REFORM—(Extensions of Remarks—June 14, 2004)

[Page: E1101]

SPEECH OF
HON. MIKE ROSS
OF ARKANSAS
IN THE HOUSE OF REPRESENTATIVES
MONDAY, JUNE 14, 2004

- Mr. ROSS. Mr. Speaker, I want to express the need for discussion on true immigration reform.

- With over eight million illegal immigrants in the U.S., and approximately half a million more entering the U.S. annually, it is now time for Congress to be diligent in trying to truly engage in discussion on how we can effectively manage immigration here in the U.S.

- I do not support illegal immigration. I also do not support amnesty for undocumented immigrants. Individuals who violate America's laws should not be rewarded for illegal behavior, and I believe amnesty perpetuates illegal immigration. The fact that there are eight million undocumented immigrants estimated to live in the U.S. illustrates alone that previous amnesty programs have not worked.

- I am seeing the effects of immigration with regards to healthcare and our hospitals. This burden is not a problem because of illegal immigration alone. Legal immigrants are working citizens, but many do not have benefits such as health insurance. They are forced to ignore health problems until they're magnified and eventually forced to seek care in emergency rooms. Unfortunately, hospitals, taxpayers, and private insurance policy holders often absorb these costs through higher premiums.

- We are appropriating funds to deal with issues such as these in the short-term, but we also have to start having discussions on long-term solutions to legal and illegal immigration. Being uninsured is only part of the problem.

- We must not lose sight of the significant role immigration has played in the development of the United States. We must be wise as we move into unchartered waters regarding new immigration policies. We must look for ways to construct positive steps that will ultimately lead to a better life for everyone.

Congressional Record article 3 of 50

CONCERNS ABOUT THE EFFECTS OF IMMIGRATION AND FOREIGN LABOR ON DOMESTIC EMPLOYMENT—(Extensions of Remarks—May 07, 2004)

[Page: E786]

SPEECH OF
HON. PAUL E. KANJORSKI
OF PENNSYLVANIA
IN THE HOUSE OF REPRESENTATIVES
THURSDAY, MAY 6, 2004

- Mr. KANJORSKI. Mr. Speaker, I rise today to address an issue about which many of my constituents are increasingly concerned: namely, the effects of immigration and foreign labor on our domestic job markets.

- It is no secret that the American economy has lost 2.6 million jobs since President Bush first took office in 2001. My home state of Pennsylvania has been one of the hardest hit in this area, losing over 135,000 manufacturing jobs in the last three years.

- This destructive trend has also begun to expand into other sectors of our economy as companies seeking to cut costs have started shifting engineering, technology, and other service-related jobs to places such as China, India, and the Philippines. Moreover, my constituents are increasingly troubled by the decisions of many American employers to bring foreign workers to the United States in record numbers. As a result of these developments, many Americans are either losing their jobs to cheap foreign labor, both at home and abroad, or are accepting lower wages due to the huge influx of domestic foreign workers, both legal and illegal.

- In these matters, I am very concerned about the failure to enforce effectively our immigration policies and prevent illegal immigration. In addition to the millions of legal immigrants already residing in the United States, experts now estimate that ten to fifteen million additional illegal immigrants now live here with roughly another 500,000 added yearly. The huge increase of foreign workers moving to the U.S. in recent decades has occurred because of our weak and shortsighted immigration policies.

- Mr. Speaker, our immigrant heritage, in my view, has helped to make the United States the greatest nation in the world. It is, however, at least equally, if not more important, that we do all we can to protect American workers, citizens, and taxpayers from the costs and potential security risks associated with illegal immigration. The President's recent proposal on immigration unfortunately falls considerably short of achieving real reform. Consequently, the

Congress needs to rethink our immigration policies and develop a long-term, workable plan for addressing these important matters.

- While I support keeping an appropriate level of legal immigration, we must put an immediate halt to our tacit approval of those who flaunt our laws and come here illegally. We must also ensure that a sufficient number of temporary work visas are available in selected areas, such as nursing, agriculture, and tourism, but only where an adequate supply of domestic workers is not available. Finally, we must ensure that current American workers are not losing their jobs or being forced to survive on depressed wages because we are voluntarily importing far more foreign workers than we need through legal and illegal immigration.

- In sum, Mr. Speaker, we need to restore the balance between protecting American workers and promoting effective immigration policy. We must also correct our flawed immigration policies in order to protect national security and promote economic growth at home for the benefit of both current U.S. workers and future generations of Americans.

Congressional Record article 4 of 50

IMMIGRATION REFORM—(Extensions of Remarks—June 08, 2004)

[Page: E1064]

SPEECH OF
HON. SAM GRAVES
OF MISSOURI
IN THE HOUSE OF REPRESENTATIVES
TUESDAY, JUNE 8, 2004

- Mr. GRAVES. Mr. Speaker, I rise today still afraid for our Nation's security. Not because of terror alerts, but because our borders remain porous. The enforcement of our immigration policy is impotent, resulting in a continued flood of illegal immigrants across our borders.

- It is time for the federal government to stop letting unchecked mass immigration undermine the wages, safety, and benefits in one occupation after another. It is time for the federal government to moderate immigration and to treat American workers, citizen and immigrant, with the respect they deserve.

- Our constituents did not elect us to help cheapen the quality of their lives by importing foreign workers at six to eight times the historical average. There is no getting around the fact that when we cheapen labor with unchecked illegal immigration, we cheapen our neighbors, both citizens and immigrants alike.

- If we moderate immigration in the context of an historical average, we will remain the most open society in the world, and begin to halt America's slide from a middle class, to a poverty class, society.

- I call on my colleagues to join me in working to reform our immigration policies and to halt the cheapening of America's citizen and immigrant workers. Without real immigration reform, our borders will not be safe and our citizens will be at risk.

Congressional Record article 6 of 50

IMMIGRATION POLICY—(Extensions of Remarks—May 19, 2004)
[Page: E909]

SPEECH OF
HON. STEVE KING
OF IOWA
IN THE HOUSE OF REPRESENTATIVES
WEDNESDAY, MAY 19, 2004

- Mr. KING of Iowa. Mr. Speaker, I wholly support an immigration policy designed to enhance the economic, social and cultural well being of the United States of America. I am looking forward to working on immigration policy as a member of the Subcommittee on Immigration, Border Security, and Claims. I intend to carry out the responsibility for crafting the immigration and naturalization policy that was delegated to Congress by our Constitution.

- Immigrants have made, and will continue to make, a valuable contribution to our Nation. I will work to develop an immigration policy that aids in the assimilation of newcomers by ensuring that the United States does not admit more immigrants than it can reasonably accommodate. Assimilation is valuable to immigrants who benefit from our shared American culture of personal responsibility, freedom and patriotism. The values shared by our civilization, founded on a heritage of western civilization, religious freedom and free enterprise capitalism, serve immigrants and native born alike. I am concerned that the recent rise in immigration levels in this country will make it difficult for newcomers to assimilate and find jobs. We must ensure cultural continuity for our great Nation.

- As Americans, we should promote a naturalization process that promotes American values, the responsibilities of citizenship and our constitutional principles. We must be careful to admit only as many newcomers as we can accommodate with jobs so that our society will not be burdened by unemployed immigrants.

- Candidates for naturalization should be proficient in the English language. Not only will English proficiency help newcomers attain better paying jobs, it also provides a means of communication with all Americans. For this reason, I have recently introduced the English Language Unity Act of 2003, H.R. 997 to declare English the official language of the United States.

- Finally, as a sovereign nation, we must control our borders. We must ensure that terrorists do not infiltrate the United States. We must tighten and strengthen border control efforts so that illegal immigrants do not enter our country. I support elimination of the visa lottery, which gives randomly selected individuals visas, when many law abiding would-be immigrants are waiting to have their applications approved. I am also concerned about the enforcement of immigration laws within our borders.

- I hope that this Congress will be vigilant in our oversight of the enforcement of existing immigration laws and make necessary changes to existing laws.

Congressional Record article 10 of 50

ADDRESSING OUR OUTDATED IMMIGRATION LAWS AND POLICIES—
(House of Representatives—March 31, 2004)

[Page: H1746]

(Mr. BARRETT of South Carolina asked and was given permission to address the House for 1 minute.)

Mr. BARRETT of South Carolina. Mr. Speaker, I rise today to thank President Bush for recognizing the need to address our outdated immigration laws and policies, as well as to urge Congress to make this issue a top priority.

First, let me start by making it clear that I believe America should always honor its immigration tradition and legally admit a reasonable number of new immigrants every year. But the tragic events of September 11 awakened most Americans to the fact that our immigration system is not only seriously flawed; it also poses a danger to our national security.

The SAFER Act would strengthen our borders with increased screening and tracking of immigrants, enhanced enforcement of the Immigration and Nationality Act, expedited removal proceedings, and reduced excessive immigration.

I also support H.R. 775, the bill of the gentleman from Virginia (Mr. Goodlatte), which would end the visa lottery system.

Our Nation is out of control. Immigration policies expose us to an increased risk of another terrorist attack, something I cannot sit back and allow to happen. It is time for Congress to act now to protect America's interests.

IMMIGRATION PROBLEMS—(House of Representatives—July 09, 2003)

[Page: H6455]

The SPEAKER pro tempore (Mr. *Gerlach*). Under the Speaker's announced policy of January 7, 2003, the gentleman from Colorado (Mr. *Tancredo*) is recognized for one-half of the remaining time until midnight, or, by the Chair's calculation, 37 1/2 minutes.

Mr. TANCREDO. Mr. Speaker, I appreciate the opportunity to address the House this evening on an issue of concern I think to me and to many people in this country.

The best way to introduce the topic I think is to discuss what happened here on this floor not too long ago when, on June 24, I offered an amendment to the Homeland Security appropriations bill that would have prohibited any appropriated funds from going to any city that has an official policy of prohibiting its police officers from cooperating with immigration law enforcement. Such policies are in clear violation of existing Federal law, yet that amendment was defeated.

It was really one of the most bizarre episodes I think that I have been involved with since I have been in the Congress, when you propose a measure that simply says that the States and cities in this country should actually abide by the law, and, that if they do not, there would be some penalty attached to the violation of that law. That is really all it said. And yet the amendment failed.

Now, let me back up and explain a little more about this whole thing and how it occurred, because it tells us something about where we are, I think, as a Nation, certainly where we are as a Congress, in our attempts to try and bring some sanity to the issue of immigration and immigration reform. We are a long way from that desired goal.

Let us start with this. The Federal law being violated by cities is section 642(a) of the 1996 Illegal Immigration Reform and Immigrant Responsibility Act. A long title. It says the following: "Notwithstanding any other provision of Federal, State or local law, a Federal, State or local government entity or official may not prohibit or in any way restrict any government entity or official from sending to or receiving from the Immigration and Naturalization Service information regarding the citizenship or immigration status, lawful or unlawful, of any individual."

Now, that is a lot of words. That is the legalese way of saying the following: Look, the Federal Government operates immigration policy for the lands.

That is our unique constitutional role. The State governments, city governments do not have any responsibility and have no authority to get involved with immigration policy.

You can certainly argue, and I do, that the Federal Government has been AWOL, if you will, on enforcing its own laws, and that is undeniably true. But that does not really in any way, shape or form, give leave to cities and States across the Nation to develop their own immigration policies, which is exactly what has been happening.

So this law that was put in place in 1996 says, you know what, States, cities? You cannot do that. You cannot establish your own immigration policy.

Now, the amendment that I was going to offer that evening was an amendment to the Homeland Security Act; it was the appropriations bill for homeland security. It was an amendment that simply applied if a State is in fact violating this law. Again, I have to go back and say this law is on the books today. I did not create it. I was not even here in the Congress when it was passed. But it is on the books.

There is one tiny problem with this law, and that is that there is no enforcement mechanism. So it says you should not do this, but, of course, there is nothing that is bad that will happen to you, city, State, locality, if you violate the law.

So I was going to take the opportunity during the passage of the Homeland Security appropriations bill to say that we are going to put some teeth into this law, and that if in fact a State or local government violates the law, they should pay some penalty; that we in fact as a Congress should say to the Nation that the laws of the Nation should be upheld. That was it, pure and simple.

Now, as I say, I knew at the time that the amendment would probably not pass, and I was not surprised by its defeat. But it is important for this body and the Congress to understand what is at stake when we talk about these so-called sanctuary policies and the impact of these policies on public safety.

Now, let me explain what sanctuary policies are and sanctuary cities. Cities across the land, because of local pressure, because of a variety of reasons, have passed laws, statutes, provisions that restrict their own employees specifically and often the police departments from sharing information with the INS. They say if you in fact stop or arrest someone and determine that that person is here illegally, you cannot tell the INS about that. You cannot aid the Immigration and Naturalization Service in upholding the law and enforcing the law, telling actual police departments to not aid in the enforcement of our law. This is bizarre, it is incredible, but it is happening. And they call themselves sanctuary cities.

Some of these cities, by the way, actually allow people to vote, even if they are not citizens of the United States, even if they are here illegally. All they require is that you show some proof of residency in that city. That is all. Bring your utility bill and you can vote. There are places in Maryland, there are places up and down the East Coast. Again, pretty bizarre stuff, but absolutely true.

Now, this House and this Congress must act to bring these cities and other jurisdictions into compliance with the law. That is why I will continue to offer this amendment on other legislation. A recent Zagby poll revealed that over 70 percent of Americans wanted our immigration laws enforced. I assure you that the same Americans want criminal immigrants off the streets and out of our country.

My amendment did not require any city to do anything other than obey existing Federal law. More than a dozen major cities and the State of Oregon are now acting in open violation and defiance of the 1996 Illegal Immigration Reform and Immigration Control Act. These cities are Los Angeles; San Francisco; San Jose; San Diego; Seattle; Houston; Durango, Colorado; Chicago; Portland, Maine; and Portland, Oregon. These cities and the State of Oregon have adopted official policies ordering law enforcement officials to not obey the law.

Can you believe that? Let me repeat it. The leaders in these cities take an oath of office just like every Member of this body, a solemn oath to support and

[Page: H6456]

defend the Constitution of the United States and to uphold the laws of the land. Yet these same local officials are directing their law enforcement officers to ignore the Federal law and to not cooperate or communicate with immigration authorities.

Now, I can understand the argument that is heard from some local officials and indeed from some law enforcement leaders. They say a city does not want to have its police officers using all their time to assist immigration officers in locating and arresting every single illegal alien residing in their locality. In many cities, the local police would have no time left for routine law enforcement or apprehending thieves, murderers or rapists. I can understand that concern, and I can understand them blaming the Federal Government for allowing so many illegal immigrants to enter this country.

But all the amendment said that I introduced, all it said was that cities could not prohibit its law enforcement officers from contacting and cooperating with immigration authorities. The amendment does not require every local police officer to call the Bureau of Immigration and Customs Enforcement for every arrest or traffic stop. In fact, my amendment does not require anyone to do anything. It merely says cities cannot prohibit their law enforcement officers from communicating with the Bureau of Immigration and Customs Enforcement when they see a valid law enforcement reason for doing so.

Local law enforcement officers need to have that freedom to access and use immigration data in the performance of their routine duties. We are not suggesting that local police departments become mere adjuncts of the immigration service. We are, however, suggesting that law enforcement agencies do have an obligation under existing Federal law to identify criminal immigrants and turn them over to the immigration authorities for deportation.

Why is this so important? It is important because over 80,000 criminal immigrants are at large, and these sanctuary laws prevent local police from apprehending these criminals until after they have committed another crime.

I am not talking now about all of the 9 to 13 million illegal immigrants in the country. I am only talking about the illegal immigrants who are already on the ICE list. ICE is the acronym for Bureau of Immigration and Custom Enforcement. They are on the ICE list for deportation.

I am only talking about the approximately 375,000 absconders, immigrants who are here illegally, who have been issued a final order for removal, that is deportation, by a Federal judge. Those names are now on the ICE immigration violators file, and that information is now available to law enforcement officers through the NCIC database, the National Criminal Information Center, which all law enforcement agencies use.

I am most concerned about the 80,000 illegal immigrants on this list of absconders who have been ordered deported because they have already committed crimes against our citizens. Why should local law enforcement officers be told by politicians to not identify these people when they come across them in the course of their routine duties? Why should local law enforcement officers not arrest and detain these criminals before they can commit another crime?

I think law enforcement does want these people to get off the streets. It is the politicians who are putting handcuffs on them, and it is up to us to remove those handcuffs.

Cities that have these policies are showing contempt, not only for Federal immigration law. They are showing contempt for the rights of their own citizens and for the citizens of neighboring towns and villages. They are saying in effect we care more about the rights of criminal immigrants than the rights of our own citizens.

Let me tell you how this practice works. When a police officer, sheriff's deputy, or State highway patrolman makes a traffic stop or otherwise has cause to question an individual whom he suspects of committing a crime, the officer routinely runs the individual's name through his on-board computer.

Now, through this computer he has an instant access to the National Criminal Justice Database, called the NCIC that I mentioned before. If there is a criminal warrant outstanding for this person's arrest from any agency elsewhere, either Federal, State or local, the person is normally arrested and booked.

With regard to identifying criminal immigrants subject to deportation, until recently a law enforcement officer would have to place a telephone call to the INS data center, law enforcement support center, and the center would tell the officer if the individual's name is on the INS detainer list. A detainer is an official request from one law enforcement agency to another that the person be held in custody. In a sanctuary city the police would not be allowed to make that call to the center, and the criminal alien would go free.

Now, the good news is that very soon the police officer or deputy will not have to make that separate call. Information will be in the computer via the NCIC. Moreover, local jurisdictions can get partial reimbursement for the cost of holding the illegal alien in a jail through a Federal program called SCAAP, all these acronyms, I am sorry for that, the State Criminal Alien Assistance Program.

The sanctuary city phenomenon presents an amazing paradox. Under our legal system, under the rule of recall that is the bedrock principle of our Nation, any person of any rank or any amount of wealth can be arrested if he has a warrant outstanding. A Congressman? Yes. A nationally renowned sports hero? Yes. A veteran who holds the Medal of Honor? Yes.

If there is a warrant outstanding, each of these citizens is subject to arrest by the lowest ranking police officer in any jurisdiction of this Nation. But in any city that has a so-called sanctuary policy, if you are an illegal alien with a felony record and a deportation order signed by a judge, you will not be questioned about your immigration status and you will not be arrested.

[Time: 23:00]

This is incredible. It is just absolutely unbelievable. But it is the state of affairs in this country.

If you are an ordinary, tax-paying citizen of Portland, Oregon, or Chicago, or Houston, and you fail to make a court appearance, you will have an FTA on your record, and you will be arrested for failure to appear. But if you are an illegal alien who has committed two felonies and are under a detainer from Immigration and Customs because of your criminal activity, you will not be arrested. If you are stopped and questioned in these cities, the police officer is not allowed to communicate with ICE to find the information or use that information.

Why is this so important? It is important because there are over 80,000 criminal immigrants loose on our streets, and these sanctuary laws prevent local police from apprehending these criminals until after they have committed another crime.

Now, I am not talking now about all of the 9 million to 13 million immigrants in the country illegally; I am only talking about the illegal immigrants who are already on the ICE list for deportation. I am tonight talking only about the approximately 375,000 absconder immigrants who are here illegally and who have been issued a final order for removal; that is, deportation by a Federal judge. Those names are on the ICE immigration violators file, and that information is now available to law enforcement through the NCIC. I am most concerned with the 80,000 illegal immigrants on the list of absconders who have been ordered deported because they have already committed crimes against our citizens.

Now, the shocking truth is that there are tens of thousands of criminal felons serving jail or prison time in these sanctuary cities who will not be turned over to ICE because the political leaders of those cities have a policy that law enforcement cannot cooperate with the INS and cannot share information with immigration authorities. Criminals will be released instead of being picked up by ICE and deported. This will happen not because ICE does not have the resources to detain them; that happens too often in too many places, but that is another issue. It will happen because the politicians in those cities have determined that this is a politically correct thing to do.

[Page: H6457]

Now, I am coming to a very important point about the numbers. There are two different numbers we need to understand when talking about illegal immigrants who are criminals and subject to deportation. Again, the number 80,000 that most lawmakers and I have been using for the past year is not a true number of illegal immigrants who are dangerous criminals. The 80,000 number is the number of felons among the approximately 375,000 individuals on the INS absconders list. But, tens of thousands of illegal immigrants with felony convictions are released from State and local correctional facilities every year and never get on the absconder list. They are theoretically placed on a detainer list, but these people are not always picked up after they are released from jail. This happens because there is a tragic lack of coordination between correctional authorities and ICE. This is a gap in our criminal justice system, and it must be fixed as quickly as possible.

To paint the picture in the cleanest possible terms, I have collected the following data from several State penal systems. Here are the estimated numbers of illegal immigrants in some of the State correctional facilities of a few States with these sanctuary cities. California prison population, 160,000; estimated illegal, 18,697. Colorado, illegal immigrants out of a population of 18,000 in prison: 748. It goes on like that. The percentage of prisoners who are illegal immigrants with detainers in these 6 States ranges from 4 percent in the States of Washington to 11.6 percent in California. The weighted average is about 9 percent. If the percentage is adjusted for the documented INS undercount of deportable immigrants, the percentage is 50 percent higher. Thus, the average percentage of illegal immigrants in our State prison population in these States is about 14.5 percent. That means that for the country as a whole, it is safe to say that at least 10 percent of the Nation's State prison population consists of deportable criminal immigrants.

When these criminals are released from incarceration, they are subject to deportation, and when identified by the INS, their names are placed on the detainer list. The problem is that this does not always happen, as I say, and, in fact, it happens less than 50 percent of the time. Thus, the alarming reality is that at the present time, thousands of these criminal immigrants are released back into our society and will not be deported until they commit another crime, if even then. There is no effective system in place to take them into custody as they finish their prison terms and deport them. In other words, the absconder list neither contains the thousands of additional criminal immigrants who have detainers, but have not yet had a hearing and received a final order to qualify them for the absconder list, nor the additional thousands of criminal immigrants who have never made it onto the detainer list in the first place.

Fortunately, there is some good news. The Bureau of Immigration and Customs Enforcement is now implementing a new database management system that will close the gap between the NCIC database for criminals and the immigration database for illegal immigrants who have been ordered deported. The NCIC system used by local law enforcement will now include the names of criminal immigrants from the immigration violators file and the Bureau of Immigration and Customs Enforcement. If the name of the individual is in the immigration violator's file, it will also be in the NCIC. The officer can then arrest and detain the illegal alien as a criminal whom a judge has ordered deported. The police officer will not need to place a separate telephone call to the immigration system and waste precious minutes or hours waiting for a reply. Information will be right there at his fingertips through the NCIC.

As I explained, there is a huge gap in the system for identifying criminal immigrants and getting them listed into the NCIC database. Whether those gaps are policy

0-595-32711-7